To Julian Alice

Good reading

Thomas Buckley

PENIKESE

Island
of
Hope

One of the Elizabeths
A Massachusetts Historical Site

By I. Thomas Buckley

edited by
Meg B. Springer

Production and Design:
Stony Brook Publishing & Productions

Production and design: Stony Brook Publishing & Productions
Greg O'Brien, editor; Bill DeLorey, executive editor for Penikese Project
Cover design by Joe Gallante, Stony Brook Publishing & Productions
Printed at: Graphic Illusions

ISBN number(soft cover): 1-887086-06-4
ISBN number(hard cover): 1-887086-07-2

Second Printing, with corrections November, 1997

Massachusetts Historical Site

The Massachusetts Historical Commission is responsible for listing and protecting the state's historical interests. In 1977, the commission listed Penikese Island in its inventory of historical assets of the Commonwealth. This action draws attention to the historical importance of the area and particularly Penikese Island. It also seeks to prevent any state agency from making significant alterations to the island.

This book is dedicated to the memory of the patients of the Penikese Island Leprosarium, the heroes and heroines that nursed them, and to their relatives and friends that also suffered in many, many ways.

Acknowledgments

Without the assistance of dedicated archivists, curators, and librarians of the following institutions, this publication would not have been possible.

Sturgis Library, Barnstable, Massachusetts
State House Library, Boston, Massachusetts
Massachusetts Archives Department, Boston, Massachusetts
Harvard University, Cambridge, Massachusetts
Dukes County Historical Society, Edgartown, Massachusetts
New Bedford Public Library, New Bedford, Massachusetts
Francis A. Countway Library of Medicine, Boston, Massachusetts
United States Public Health Service Gillis W. Long Hansen's Disease
    Center, Carville, Louisiana
Division of Fisheries and Wildlife, Westboro, Massachusetts
Old Dartmouth Historical Society, New Bedford Whaling Museum,
    New Bedford, Massachusetts
Marine Biological Laboratories, Woods Hole, Massachusetts

Individuals who assisted greatly are:
George Cadwalader, Penikese Island School
David Masch, Penikese Island School
John Burk, Smith College, Northampton, Massachusetts
Janet Bosworth, Cuttyhunk, Massachusetts
Clair Baisly, Chatham, Massachusetts
Alice Dobbyn, Chatham, Massachusetts
Alberta K. Byington, Sacramento, California
Robert A. Parker, Denver, Colorado
Marylyn Sturdivant, Golden Meadow, Louisiana
Eric Linder, Chatham, Massachusetts
Leontine L. Barros, Medford, Massachusetts
Dorothy D. Reiss Barros, Medford, Massachusetts

In addition, there were scores of others who assisted in the publication of this book. I am grateful to them all.

Table of Contents

Illustrations and Photographs

Photographs from 1925 to 1938 courtesy of the Massachusetts Division of Fisheries and Wildlife, reproduced by Abbot Rogers of North Chatham, Massachusetts.

Author's Note

Penikese, a tiny island off the southeast coast of Massachusetts, is the northernmost isle of the Elizabeth Island chain. Penikese lies at 41° 27' north latitude and 70° 55' longitude, one mile north of Cuttyhunk Island and 14 miles southwest of Cape Cod. This island—situated in Buzzards Bay, in Gosnold Township, of Dukes County—is a little known place, and yet it has affected the lives of thousands of people.

From the start, Penikese was populated by independent island people that loved the land and eked out a living there—fishermen, farmers, and ship pilots.

In 1873, the John Anderson School was built there, a school for naturalist teachers. Instructors were internationally known. The school closed after the second summer session.

In 1905, the Commonwealth opened a special hospital on Penikese for the treatment of people with leprosy (called Hansen's disease today). The hospital operated for 16 years, with the hope that a cure for leprosy would eventually be found.

It is my hope in publishing this book that readers will get a better understanding of the suffering and devastation caused by this disease, and with this new knowledge, may have a kinder outlook towards its victims.

There is a small graveyard on Penikese where many of the patients are buried. It is also my hope that, as the family of Isabelle Barros has done, some reader will recognize an ancestor, find the burial site and place a stone on the unmarked grave.

Today the island is occupied by a school for adjudicated teenage boys. The program strives to return these youths to society as productive persons.

I. Thomas Buckley

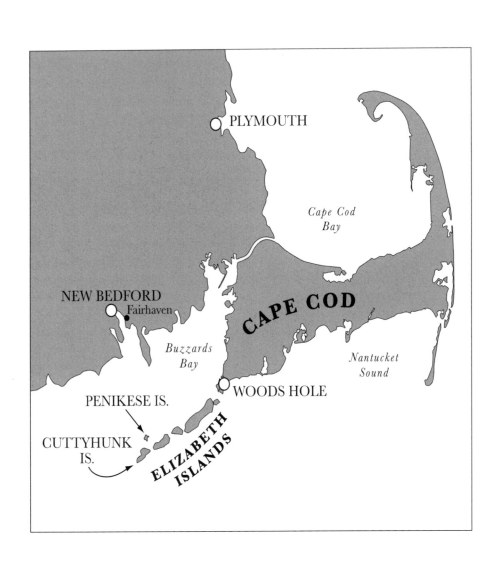

PLYMOUTH

Cape Cod
Bay

CAPE COD

NEW BEDFORD
Fairhaven

Buzzards
Bay

Nantucket
Sound

WOODS HOLE

PENIKESE IS.

CUTTYHUNK
IS.

ELIZABETH
ISLANDS

1
The Formation of
the Elizabeth Islands

Indian Legend

The Elizabeth Islands, a string of fragile islands in Buzzards Bay off the coast of Cape Cod and New Bedford, were created by a giant named Maushop, says a Wampanoag Indian legend. He was a good friend to the Cape Cod Indians.

One day the Indians asked Maushop for help in ridding the Cape of the Pukwudgees—little people who grew no taller than ten inches and continually annoyed the Indians. The Pukwudgees broke the Indians' arrows, poked holes in their canoes, and placed dry sticks under the Indians' feet while they hunted.

Maushop agreed to help. He and his five sons crawled through the swamps and fields looking for the Pukwudgees, but the wise Pukwudgees had discovered the plan and crept up behind Maushop's sons, blinding them with their magic and killing them with bows and arrows.

Sadly, Maushop carried his sons to Buzzards Bay to bury them, covering their bodies with mounds of soil and rock, on which he planted trees and grass. Soon, the ocean's waters rose and separated the mounds, creating the islands we now know as the Elizabeths—places like Naushon, Pasque, Nashawena, Cuttyhunk, and Penikese.

After the death of his sons, the good giant Maushop became lonely. The last anyone saw of him, says the legend, Maushop was walking south. No one knows for certain what became of him.[1]

Since the Wampanoags had no written language, they used storytelling to entertain and instruct their children. For hundreds of years, they passed down this tale from generation to generation, and believed it was true.

While the Wampanoags told a compelling story of this beloved giant who created the Cape and Islands, a well-known scientist in the late 1800s developed a theory about snow and ice. Many years after the arrival of Europeans to this country, Louis Agassiz,* a Swiss naturalist, presented the idea of the existence of a universal glacial era, commonly called the Glacial Theory.

Glacial Theory

"Glaciers are composed of different materials according to the positions selected for investigation. On the mountain tops they are mere snow fields; deeper they are composed of ice crystals, the ice becoming more compact as you go downward until the bottom is clear solid ice.… Glaciers possess a motion in themselves which is both upward and a downward motion; it is the greatest in the middle and least upon the edges. Moving ice therefore exerts a great power. As a glacier moves, it collects a large quantity of loose materials which it carries along with it.… The bottoms of glaciers, then, being covered with rocks, act like an immense rasp."[2]

Louis Agassiz, 1873
Lecture delivered on Penikese Island
(Anderson School of Natural History)

There are a number of theories on how and when Cape Cod and its offshore islands were formed. Most geologists agree on the basics, which are summarized here by U.S. Geological Survey geologist Robert Oldale in *A Guide to Nature on Cape Cod and the Islands*:

"The Laurentide Ice Sheet, the last of the great ice age glaciers in North America, began to form in Canada about 75,000 years ago, at the beginning of the Wisconsinan Glacial Stage. For much of the Wisconsinan Stage, the Laurentide ice sheet was mostly confined within the borders of Canada, but about 25,000 years ago it advanced into New England, and reached the Cape and Islands about 21,000 years ago. Here, in a more moderate temperature climate, the advance stopped. Thereafter, the retreat began, as melting at the glacier margin exceeded the rate of ice advance. As the glacier advanced, it scraped up soil and loose sediments and gouged and plucked fragments of the solid rock that lay beneath the ice. These materials were carried forward in the base of the ice and deposited along the glacier margin to form moraines, or carried beyond the edge of the ice by meltwater streams to form outwash

*Agassiz later became the founder of the John Anderson School on Penikese Island.

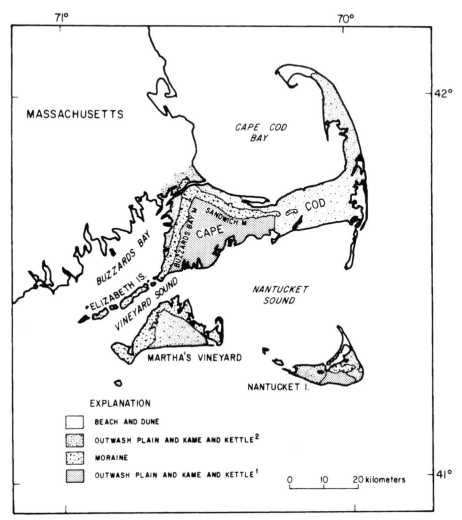

Generalized geologic map of the Cape and Islands, showing the distribution and relative age of the moraines and outwash plains, and the distribution of beach and dune: #1—outwash plains and kame and kettle terrain older than the adjacent moraine; #2—outwash plains and kame and kettle terrain younger than the adjacent moraine.

Illustration courtesy of the United States Geological Survey

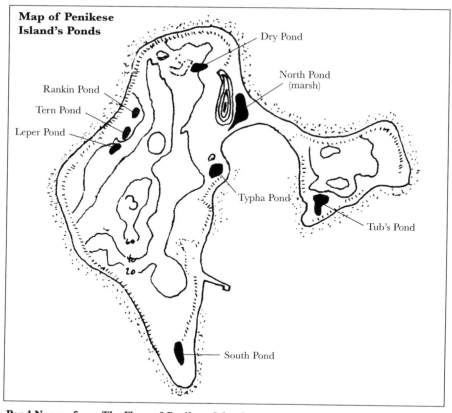

Map of Penikese Island's Ponds

Dry Pond

North Pond (marsh)

Rankin Pond

Tern Pond

Leper Pond

Typha Pond

Tub's Pond

South Pond

**Pond Names from *The Flora of Penikese Island.*
Scott Lauermann and C. John Burk.**

plains. These landforms characterize the glacial Cape and Islands.

"The glacial deposits on the islands of Martha's Vineyard and Nantucket were laid down earliest, at the maximum extent of the ice, and those on the Elizabeth Islands and Cape Cod were deposited somewhat after the Laurentide ice sheet had begun its retreat. At the close of the Wisconsinan Glacial Stage, the great continental glaciers retreated throughout the Northern Hemisphere, and water—formerly trapped in ice on the continents—returned to the ocean, where sea level began to rise."

Today, the island of Penikese is much smaller than when it was formed. For centuries wind, rain, and waves have eroded the island, whittling it to about 75 acres.* The glacier left behind five huge blocks of ice that melted to form small ponds called kettle holes. Today, we

*This natural process of erosion continues today and the island is ever so slowly being washed away.

know them as Typha Pond, Dry Pond, Leper Pond, Tern Pond, and Rankin Pond.*[3]

The glacier also left behind conglomerates—boulders consisting of a mass of pebbles naturally cemented together by clay. The largest is approximately five feet high and six feet wide. These conglomerates, geologists speculate, may have come from the Middleboro, Massachusetts area.

In addition to conglomerates, large bedrock boulders—dragged down with the glacier—are found on the island. The largest such boulder, or glacial erratic, is called "The Plow" because it looks like one; it measures 16 feet high, 25 feet wide, and 39 feet long. It is slightly smaller than Doane (Enos) Rock in Eastham on the Cape, which is the largest boulder in southern New England.[4]

*There are three other ponds on the island that are not kettle holes: The Marsh (or North Pond), Tubs Pond, and South Pond. These were probably formed by the coalescing of beaches. All the ponds and kettle holes on Penikese now have brackish water (a mixture of salt water and fresh water) most of the year, and often dry up in the summer. Dry Pond, however, is dry most of the time.

2
Early Explorers
and Indians (1003-1675)

Early Explorers

Viking sagas vary greatly. Many historians, however, agree that in the year 1003, Leif Eriksson left Greenland to explore North America, seeking land suitable for occupation. Eriksson and his crew explored several locations before discovering "Vinland"—an area some historians believe to be the coast of southeastern New England. If this is true, Eriksson may have used Nomans Land, an island south of Martha's Vineyard, as a base for exploration.[1] Stone foundations on the island that can be seen today are believed to be the remains of Vikings' booths (or dwellings). While there is no evidence of Viking occupation on any of the Elizabeth Islands, Norsemen most likely visited them.

After Eriksson and his crew returned to Greenland, according to the sagas, many other Vikings followed his Vinland route for further exploration. Eriksson never set foot on Vinland again, but allowed his booths to be used by others. During an exploration in 1010, a child by the name of Snorri Karlsefeson was born there. The boy may have been the first white child born in North America.[2]

The last Viking expedition to Vinland in 1015 and 1016 established a more permanent settlement. But during this expedition, Eriksson's sister, Freydis, and one of the group leaders were jealous of other leaders, and had them and their followers slain. When the group returned to Greenland with word of the killings, the Vikings refused to authorize more expeditions to Vinland.

During the next four centuries, visitors to the New England area—it is widely believed—were fishermen from the Azores, Ireland, and the Arctic. Recorded voyages began with John Cabot, an Italian explorer who lived in England. In 1498, Cabot and his son, Sabastian, sailed from Labrador along the New England coast to Maryland. In 1524, Giovanni da Verrazano, a Florentine explorer, voyaged from Newfoundland to New York Bay. And in 1542,

Jehan Alefonce, a French navigator, sailed from Canada to Massachusetts Bay.

The first recorded visit to Penikese was made in 1602 by Bartholomew Gosnold. Captain Gosnold left Falmouth, England on March 26, 1602 with a crew of 32 men aboard a small bark named *The Concord*. The goal of the voyage was to establish a settlement in Virginia and to trade with the Indians in the New World. Two men aboard the ship, John Brereton and Gabriel Archer, recorded events of the trip, making Gosnold's expedition one of the most well-known.

Gosnold first arrived off the coast of Maine on May 14, and then sailed south, stopping at a point he named "Cape Cod" because of its abundance of codfish. He also named the island now known as Nomans Land, as "Martha's Vineyard," and named Martha's Vineyard, "Dover Cliffs." Gosnold then sailed to Cuttyhunk which he named "Elizabeth Isle,"[3] perhaps after Queen Elizabeth or his sister Elizabeth.*

Gosnold established a settlement on Cuttyhunk because of its plentiful wood supply, fresh water, and good soil. His crew built living quarters and a fort on a small island in the middle of a pond. They thought this to be a safe location in case of attack from Indians, though the local Indians had already established friendly contact.

On May 24,** Gabriel Archer wrote, "From Elizabeth Isle [Cuttyhunk] unto main is four leagues. On the north side, near adjoining unto the island, Elizabeth, is an islet in compass half a mile, full of cedars, called by me Hills hap*** [Penikese]."[4] A few days later, Gosnold and some of his men sailed to Penikese, where they found a "great stand of cedars" and a sheltered sandy cove. His arrival startled four Indians, who abandoned their canoe in the cove and ran into the woods. The explorers put the canoe aboard their boat, and left the Indians stranded.

A few weeks later, Gosnold left Gabriel Archer and a few men on Cuttyhunk, with a promise to return the following day. He then sailed to Penikese to cut some cedar trees to take back to England. After the work was completed, Gosnold explored the bay.[5]

Meanwhile, his men on Cuttyhunk were low on food, and four of

---

*The name Elizabeth Isle has been extended to include all the islands in the archipelago now known as the Elizabeth Islands.

**May 24 is Old Style and is now June 4.

***The name given to Penikese by Archer should not be confused with the island Haps Hill, which is closer to the mainland. "Hap" is an old English word meaning "fortune.".

them set out to shellfish. Two were attacked by Indians, presumably the ones from whom Gosnold had stolen the canoe. When one of the Englishmen was slightly wounded in the attack, both the Indians and the Englishmen ran in opposite directions. The two Englishmen ultimately got lost in the woods and spent the night in the swamps, while the others at the fort worried about their missing comrades. When the two men returned the next day, a straw vote was taken to go back to England. On June 13, Gosnold returned to his hungry and frightened men on Cuttyhunk, and complied with their wishes. *The Concord* was then loaded with cedar, sassafras, and the Indian canoe, and on June 17, 1602, Gosnold and his men left for England.* The canoe reportedly was put on display in a museum.

American Indians

The Indians Gosnold's men had encountered were most likely Pokanockets[6] who lived on the Elizabeth Islands. They were part of a tribe called Succanessets from the Falmouth, Cape Cod area. It is believed that some of the Indians living on the Elizabeth Islands belonged to the Gay Head tribe of Martha's Vineyard. Today, these Indians are generally known as Wampanoags, which are members of the Algonquin nation.[7]

Three of the Elizabeth Islands—Naushon, Pasque, and Nashawena—had year-round Indian settlements. In the spring and summer, the Indians lived on hilltops where the breeze would keep the insects away. During the colder months, they moved to more protected areas,[8] usually on the same island. It is not known for what purpose the Indians used the island of Cuttyhunk; however the name is a derivative of the Indian word, "Poocutohhunkunnoh."[9] No Indian campsites have ever been found on Penikese, although some artifacts have been discovered. A Wampanoag war ax was dug up in the island's cove by a shell fisherman. This ax was well-preserved and is on display at the Robbins Museum of Archaeology in Middleboro. Other artifacts include an arrowhead, a stone knife blade, and pestles. Indians may have used Penikese for hunting and fishing, but the island was probably too small for longer visits.

Penikese Island was a place of refuge for at least two Indians war-

*Captain Gosnold later returned to this country and became a prominent citizen of Jamestown, Virginia.

9

riors during King Philip's War, which began in 1675. This war was between the Wampanoag Indians and the white settlers over the use of land. Metacomet, who was the ruler of the Wampanoags, was called King Philip by the white men. The two Indians who escaped to Penikese were Tatoson, a captain of King Philip, and Tatoson's son or nephew, Penachason. These men had led an attack on a garrison house near Plymouth in which 15 white settlers were killed, and a reward of four coats was offered for each of them. Tatoson and Penachason did not stay long on the island and soon rejoined King Philip's army.[10] It is possible that Penachason named Penikese Island after himself.

3
Early Owners and Residents
of Penikese Island (1641-1867)

Thomas Mayhew and his ten-year-old son, Thomas, Jr., came to Massachusetts from England in the year 1631. Their first known residence was in Medford, where Mr. Mayhew was the agent for a wealthy English merchant, Matthew Cradock. Not only did Mayhew make a profit for his employer, but he also accumulated land, wealth, and political power for himself. Mayhew later moved to Watertown, where he owned a large farm, and continued to acquire land and local businesses.

In September, 1641, Mayhew and his son became the first white men to own Penikese Island. They received a grant from agents of the King of England, which gave them ownership of Nantucket, Martha's Vineyard, and the Elizabeth Islands. Mayhew and his son planned to make money by selling and leasing the land to settlers; they also hoped to convert the Indians to Christianity.

In 1642, at the age of 21, Thomas Mayhew, Jr. established a white settlement on Martha's Vineyard, where he was elected leader and pastor. Like his father, he was devoted to God and felt the need to bring Christianity to the Indians. He learned their customs and language and soon became a respected minister to both the Indians and settlers.

Thomas Mayhew, Sr. arrived at the settlement on Martha's Vineyard early in 1645 to act as governor and missionary. He established a court system which gave equal rights to the Indians and the white settlers. At one point he established a small Indian army. Although Mayhew owned the islands under English law, he still felt it necessary to buy the land from the Indians first, before selling it to the settlers. As a result, the settlers and Indians lived together peacefully, even when these groups were at war on the mainland.

In 1656, Thomas Mayhew, Jr. sailed for England to make a personal report to the Church's authorities about the missionary work being done with the Indians. No one knows what became of the ship he sailed on, but neither the ship nor Thomas Mayhew Jr. was ever seen again.

13

For many years after his son's presumed death, the senior Mayhew continued preaching and encouraging people to settle on Martha's Vineyard. Eventually, he sold most of his land holdings on the Elizabeth Islands. He died on March 25, 1682, just a few days before his ninetieth birthday. Lloyd Hare, noted historian and biographer, wrote of him:

> "Upon the basis of his life as an Indian missionary, the fame of Thomas Mayhew rests best...the triumph which endears him to posterity was his administration of Indian affairs... A manorial lord, a British Colonial Governor, he became one of the great missionaries of his day and one of the greatest in all ages to govern and pacify a savage race. To the Indian he was father, counselor, and ruler: "sachem" as they upon occasion called him."[1]

Daniell Wilcockes bought the islands of Penikese and Pasque from Mayhew in about 1670.[2] Wilcockes never lived on his islands, but grazed sheep there; sheep were brought to these islands in the summer for protection against wolves on the mainland. Wilcockes also harvested wood on the island. Trees were indiscriminately cut for fuel and lumber, which is why Penikese is now almost denuded of trees.

Wilcockes lived with his wife and ten children in various places around the Massachusetts and Rhode Island border. His wife, Elizabeth Cooke, was the daughter of John Cooke, a passenger on the *Mayflower*. Wilcockes ran a farm, owned hundreds of acres of land, and was a partner of a local ferry service. He was also an interpreter for his neighbor, Captain Benjamin Church, the famous Indian fighter. During King Philip's War, Wilcockes and Church persuaded the Indian Sachem, Awashonks, not to join forces with King Philip.

In 1682, Wilcockes was heavily fined for the illegal purchase of land from Indians, which was a common offense at that time. The law required that court permission be granted before settlers could buy Indian-owned land. Massachusetts Bay Colony also required all taxpayers to pay taxes to the established church. Wilcockes, who was not a member of the established church, was offended by this law and in 1692 refused to pay his taxes. He was then arrested and fined again. Without paying this fine, Wilcockes escaped to Rhode Island, where greater religious tolerance existed. In 1696, while he was still in exile in Rhode Island, Wilcockes sold Penikese Island to his neighbor, Peleg Slocum.

Years later, Wilcockes petitioned the Massachusetts Court to allow him to pay his fine and to move back to the Massachusetts Bay Colony. In his petition, Wilcockes said that he was old and poor, and that his wife had gone mad. He was allowed to return and died one year later, leaving an estate of great wealth—about 1,900 acres of land, personal property valued at 1,290 pounds, and interests in other properties.[3]

Peleg Slocum not only brought many Slocums to the Elizabeth Islands, but helped bring the Quaker faith there as well. He and his wife, Mary Holder, of Providence, lived in Dartmouth, Massachusetts while many members of his family lived on the larger Elizabeth Islands. (Nashawena, for some years, was known as "Slocum's Island.")

Slocum and his wife were zealous members of the Society of Friends and often held meetings in their spacious home in Dartmouth. When this group became too large, they and others contributed money and land to build the first Apponegansett Meeting House in Dartmouth.

Like many large landowners of his time, Peleg Slocum considered himself a farmer. However, a substantial amount of his time was spent on the affairs of the Society of Friends. He would often sail his boat to the Elizabeth Islands, Martha's Vineyard, and Nantucket to visit family and hold meetings with other Quakers, such as the famous Mary Starbuck.

When Peleg Slocum died around 1732, his land holdings in Dartmouth were over 1,000 acres. He also had interests in the islands of Nashawena, Cuttyhunk, and Penikese. For the next 70 years, various members of his large family held ownership of Penikese. It is not known how many family members actually lived on Penikese, but for some time tenant farmers occupied it.[4]

One of the tenant farmers who lived on Penikese Island, while Slocum owned it, was John Flanders. He was married to Sarah Hillman, of Chilmark, and they had six children. John Flanders was not only a farmer but a fisherman, pilot, and wrecker.[5] As a wrecker, Flanders was hired by ship owners or insurance companies to salvage vessels that had been wrecked. As a pilot, Flanders navigated ships for captains who did not know the local waters. New Bedford at this time was becoming one of the busiest seaports in the world due to the growing whaling industry. Services of a pilot were in great demand but competition between pilots remained keen. They would scan the

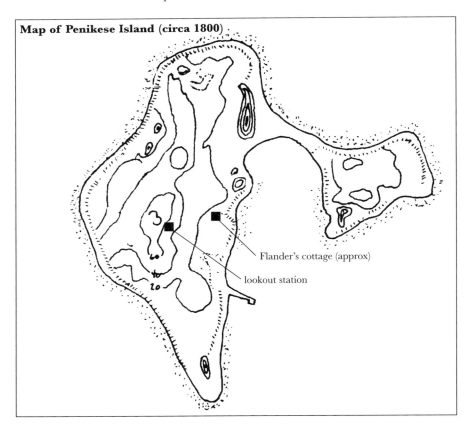

Map of Penikese Island (circa 1800)

Flander's cottage (approx)

lookout station

horizon for ships in need of a pilot; the first man to reach a vessel was usually hired.

Today on Penikese's highest hill a large curved boulder sits, surrounded by smaller stones—a perfect place to rest and watch the sea. This may have been John Flander's lookout station. The Flanders lived on Penikese for about 30 years. During this time, Penikese's ownership was transferred from the Slocum family to a man named Silas Gifford.

Silas Gifford bought the island in three sections from different Slocum families. The first section was purchased in 1800, and the second in 1804. There is no record showing when the third section was purchased. Under Gifford's ownership, life on the island continued with sheep raising, farming, fishing, and ship-piloting.

Very little is known about Silas Gifford except a few vital statistics. He was born in 1747 to Adam and Ann Gifford and, at the age of 41, married Ruth Peabody of Dartmouth. The Giffords lived on the island with two families who were tenant farmers: the Flanders, who had lived there when the Slocums had owned it; and the Grinnells, who may have also lived on the island prior to the Giffords.[6]

In 1807, Dr. James Freeman wrote an article entitled "A Description of Dukes County" for the Massachusetts Historical Society. In this article, Freeman stated that three families and 150 sheep lived on Penikese Island at that time.[7] To raise that many sheep one would need at least 75 acres of pasturage, the present size of the island. If Freeman's statement was accurate, then the island was certainly deforested by then.

Oliver C. Grinnell and his family may have moved off the island around the time the Giffords purchased their last section of Penikese. Oliver Grinnell, Jr., who claimed to have been born on Penikese in 1796, returned there in 1826, the same year Silas Gifford died. He and his wife, Sally Winslow, from Chilmark, had married the year before and went on to spend 25 years on the island. Like his father, Oliver, Jr. was a tenant farmer. The Grinnells had 12 children, seven of whom lived to maturity.[8] When the Gifford heirs sold Penikese in 1852, the Grinnells moved to the large island of Naushon.

The man who bought Penikese Island from the Gifford heirs was also named John Flanders. This name was very popular in this area during the nineteenth century; however, the life of the earlier John Flanders so parallels the life of the latter John Flanders that it is reasonable to suspect that they were father and son. For example, both men were ship pilots,[9] a job which requires many years of experience in the local waters. Flanders was probably no stranger to the island when he purchased it.

The owner John Flanders was born about 1800. He and his wife Mary and their children were Penikese Island's only residents for 13 years. In 1865, Flanders sold Penikese to Beriah Manchester for $3,000 and then moved off the island. Years later, in 1873, Flanders became caretaker of Penikese and lived there for many years in this capacity, until he drowned during a winter storm at the age of 91.[10]

When Beriah Manchester bought Penikese Island from Flanders in 1865, he had just retired from 30 years as a whaler. During his career, he sailed on various ships in many areas of both the Atlantic and Pacific oceans.[11] Between voyages in 1846 he married Phoebe Mosher, and the couple raised two sons.

Like many whalers, Manchester dreamed of owning a farm. When he moved to Penikese, he not only had a farm but operated a small fish oil factory on the island.[12] The fish oil was sold for medicinal purposes, and the by-product was sold to a fertilizer plant, The Pacific Guano Company in Woods Hole.

Perhaps Manchester tired of his farm; in 1867, two years after he bought Penikese Island, he sold it to a wealthy New Yorker, John Anderson. Being a shrewd Yankee sea captain, Manchester sold Penikese for almost three times the amount he paid for it.

After the sale, Manchester operated the pilot boat *Red, White and Blue* out of New Bedford. For a time, he tried coasting—carrying freight from New Bedford to small local seaports. Finally, he gave up the sea and spent the rest of his life on a farm outside of New Bedford. He died there at the age of 92.[13]

JOHN ANDERSON.

are furnished with every necessar
the way of aquaria, microscopes,
implements. As an illustration
the professor mentioned the case
who wanted to become a natural
handed him a piece of worn co
him a fortnight to find out

John Anderson, as he appeared in a newspaper story in *Harper's Weekly*

4
The Anderson School of Natural History (1867-1880)

After John Anderson bought Penikese Island from Beriah Manchester in 1867, he and his wife built a large house there—a retreat from the busy social and political life they led in New York City. The house, constructed by their combining and adding to several buildings already on the island, sat on a bluff about 75 yards from the east shore and, as was the custom at that time, it faced south. The Andersons also built a large barn and a sheep shed, about 200 yards north of the house, and a boathouse near the beach.[1]

Anderson was one of the most successful tobacconists in the country. He opened New York's first cigar store, and later added the city's first news-stand.[2] He also was active in New York politics and declined several offers to run for mayor and governor.[3] He was an opponent of the Boss Tweed regime, and some of the other island residents suspected him of hiding Tweed's political enemies on Penikese.

During the winter of 1872-73, Anderson read an article about the internationally-known scientist, Louis Agassiz, a highly-honored naturalist from Switzerland who, among many achievements, developed the Glacial Theory. In proving his theory, he made many expeditions to the Swiss Alps, which put him heavily in debt. To raise funds to repay these debts, Agassiz came to the United States to give lectures. He was an immediate success, sometimes drawing crowds of 3,000 in one night. Agassiz was greatly impressed by the United States and stayed to take the position of Chairman at Harvard University's new Geology and Zoology Department.*

In December, 1872, a colleague, Nathaniel Shaler, suggested to Agassiz that a summer school for teachers of natural history be estab-

*While at Harvard, Agassiz refused to hold the traditional professorial role. His students were accepted on the basis of whether he liked them or not; no entrance exams were given; and women were encouraged to attend his classes. Professor Agassiz enjoyed teaching and his classes were always well-attended. He founded the Museum of Comparative Zoology at Harvard. "The Agassiz," as it is called today, is still one of the most important zoological museums in the world.

lished in a seaside area. Agassiz liked the idea and, with no money or definite site in mind, he advertised the new summer school. This notice created a lot of interest, and stories were carried in several newspapers throughout the country. It was one of these articles that John Anderson happened to read.

Soon after this, Anderson—who gave generously to the arts and sciences—contacted Agassiz and offered the island to him, along with a $50,000 endowment. Anderson also promised to give $10,000 a year as long as the school continued.[4] Penikese Island interested Agassiz because it is part of a glacial moraine and was an ideal place for him to lecture on his Glacial Theory. Some of Agassiz's associates and his son, Alexander, advised him not to accept Anderson's offer because Penikese was too far away and transporting people and supplies would be expensive. Agassiz, however, did not agree and accepted Anderson's offer.

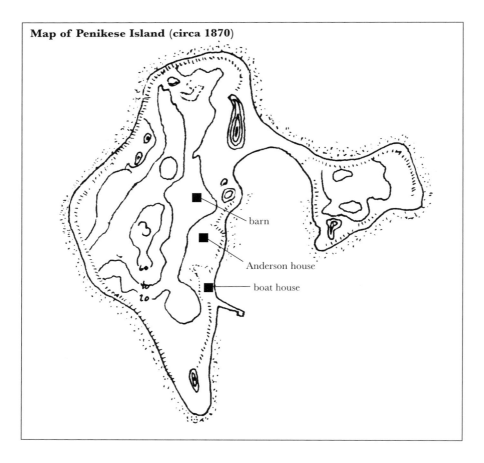

Map of Penikese Island (circa 1870)

barn

Anderson house

boat house

The Anderson House, 1890 *Photo: Marine Biological Laboratories*

On April 21, 1873, Penikese Island's ownership (except Tubs Point, which remained in Anderson's name) was transferred to Louis Agassiz's name. Two boatloads of guests arrived on the island to celebrate the occasion. Guests included educators from the New Bedford school system, friends of Agassiz from Harvard, and business associates of Mr. Anderson. One of the boats was captained by John Flanders, a former owner of Penikese, who was then the caretaker.

It was at this event that Mr. Anderson met Professor Agassiz for the first time. In Agassiz's speech that day, he announced that his summer school would be named the Anderson School of Natural History. He also announced that the school would open on July 8 of that year.[5]

With three months to build a summer school for 50 students, Agassiz quickly began making plans. A dormitory, classroom, and dining hall had to be built. Furnishings and supplies had to be ordered and purchased. Kitchen staff, instructors, and assistants had to be hired, and a course of study arranged.

Agassiz hired Boston architect Robert H. Slack to design the buildings and New Bedford area builders to erect them. These contracts were signed on May 16. Lumber was ordered from Maine and arrived in New Bedford on May 28. Because the Anderson's house was not large enough to accommodate both stone masons and carpenters, the carpenters assembled the framing in New Bedford while

23

Louis Agassiz *Photo: Marine Biological Laboratories*

the masons built the foundations on Penikese. On June 5, the carpenters arrived on Penikese and had the major part of the framing installed by June 14.

Although the workmen had worked at a feverish pace, the buildings were only partially completed when the Agassiz family and their party arrived on July 5, three days before the school was to open. The main building, which was to have laboratories on the first floor and student housing on the second, had no floors, shingles, or partitions. Nevertheless, Agassiz felt sure everything would be ready on time.

While the Agassiz party examined the buildings, many of the carpenters boarded the boat the Agassizes had arrived on and sailed home to spend the weekend. When this was discovered, an urgent appeal was made to the remaining carpenters, who were leaving the next morning, to stay and work through the weekend. There are two written accounts of this event, each attributing the plea to someone else. Dr. Burt Wilder, a friend of Agassiz, stated that it was Agassiz who persuaded the carpenters. Mrs. Agassiz, however, wrote that "Flanders... the man in charge of the Island for Mr. Anderson... made a thrilling address... to the carpenters to convince them to work all weekend." [6]

Mrs. Agassiz also wrote that she, the Wilders, their children, and a student, who had arrived early, washed four dozen plates, six dozen cups and saucers, many dozens of glasses and "fifty-six chamber sets, including all the ordinary pieces." By Sunday night, the floors had been installed in the main building. On Monday, and Tuesday morning Mrs. Agassiz and her small group unpacked furniture and arranged the dormitory floor space into "imaginary rooms" by means of "neat sets of furniture." [7]

Near noon on Tuesday, July 8, the Anderson School of Natural History opened its doors on schedule when the New Bedford steamer *Helen Augusta* arrived at the Penikese Island dock, with 80 passengers. On board were dignitaries, guests, students, and the kitchen staff. Professor Agassiz welcomed them and then gave a short tour of the island, allowing time for the kitchen staff to prepare the catered lunch they had brought.

The tour ended at the Anderson barn, which only that morning had housed cows, and now served as the dining area. Before lunch was served, Agassiz asked for a silent prayer and gave a welcome speech, an event which was immortalized by John Greenleaf Whittier in his poem, *The Prayer of Agassiz*.

Said the Master to the youth:
"We have come in search of truth,
Trying with uncertain key
Door by door of mystery;
We are reaching, through His Laws,
To the garment-hem of Cause,
Him, the endless, unbegun,
The Unnamable, the One
Light of all our light the Source
Life of life, and Force of force.

From *The Prayer of Agassiz*
By John Greenleaf Whittier

After lunch the students were shown to their "rooms," which they found far from complete. The windows had no glass and a hanging blanket separated the men's and women's quarters.[8] But because it was considered an honor to be a student of "The Master," as Agassiz was affectionately called by his students at Harvard, few complained and none quit.

Tuition was free at the Anderson School, with only a small charge for room and board. Classes were very informal and were held both indoors and out. The students roamed the beaches, dredged the harbor for specimens in *The Sprite,** and had frequent open discussions with their instructors. With the exception of guest teachers, most of the instruction was given by Louis Agassiz, Alexander Agassiz, Edwin Bicknell, and Paulus Roetter, all of Harvard University.** [9]

In the first summer session there were 16 women and 28 men from 11 different states. Agassiz worked these students long and hard. One of them wrote the following account of an average day.

> "...there was the breakfast horn, then breakfast, and the lectures, which all or part might attend, occupying that part of the forenoon not devoted to exploring, collecting or dissecting, and then dinner time. After dinner a similar routine occupied the afternoon until tea time. Sometimes we had a lecture after dark, while we often dissected by candle light. Thus we were never idle, always busy, always learning! ...and far into the night we remained rewriting our daily notes." [10]

On August 29, the Anderson School of Natural History finished its first session, and Louis Agassiz once again had astounded the educational world. He attracted the country's leading naturalists to teach students how to study nature from the environment instead of from books. Many educators thought that the school might become the greatest single influence in the teaching of natural history.***

During the summer, Agassiz had spent much of his time with his students and, with his responsibilities as President-Director,

---

*A yacht called *The Sprite* was donated by Charles G. Galloupe to the school for use as a workboat.

**The guest teachers were as follows: A. S. Packard, E. S. Morse, F. W. Putnam from the Peabody Academy of Science in Salem; Alfred Mayer from the Stevens Institute in Hoboken, New Jersey; D. Waterhouse Hawkins, a naturalist from Great Britian; D. S. Jordan, a former student of Agassiz and a naturalist from Appleton, Wisconsin; B. G. Wilder, of Cornell Universtiy; Arnold Guyot and Count L. F. dePourtales, friends of Agassiz and fellow naturalists. Packard lectured on crustaceans, Morse on mollusks, and Jordan on algae. Bicknell taught microscopical observation. (Most students had never used a microscope because they were far too expensive for the average school system to purchase.) Guyot taught physical geography, and Hawkins taught on extinct mammals. Mr. Roetter, a naturalist artist, taught the students how to draw their specimens.

***This statement later proved itself to be true.

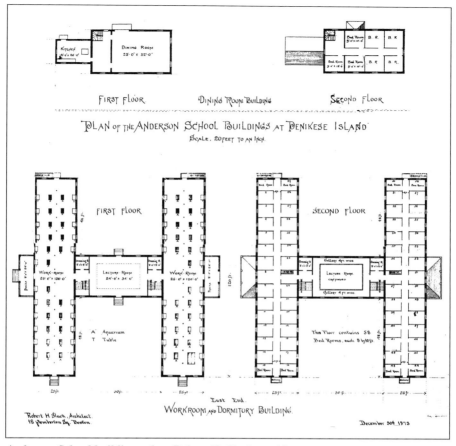

Anderson School buildings plan. Robert H. Slack, architect

he became exhausted. By the end of the summer, he was ill. Louis Agassiz never regained his health and died later that year on December 14, at the age of 66—leaving behind his wife and son, Alexander. Ten years later, his wife, Elizabeth, became the first president of Radcliffe College, a position she held for 20 years.

Arnold Guyot, a fellow naturalist and teacher on the island, wrote the following account about his friend Louis Agassiz's last month on Penikese:

"It was to me supremely touching to see the great naturalist, at Penikese, a few months before his death, devoting his last strength to a crowd of eager learners, directing them, to the exclusive study of the book of nature, and showing them, by word and deed, how to observe it, and how to be taught by these living realities."[11]

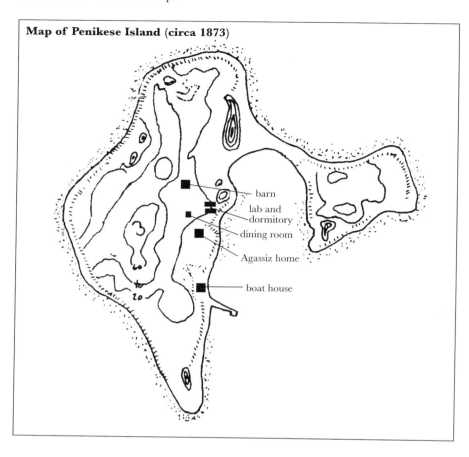

Map of Penikese Island (circa 1873)

barn

lab and
dormitory

dining room

Agassiz home

boat house

In 1874, Alexander Agassiz took on the responsibilities of President-Director and prepared for the next session that summer. The Andersons gave up whatever plans they may have had for the section of Penikese they still owned, Tubs Point, and donated it to the Anderson School.

Louis Agassiz's friends and colleagues joined Alexander on Penikese Island for the school's second session in July, 1874. The number of people who had requested admission was overwhelming and many of the students from the first year elected to return. The final selection included 20 women and 26 men. When the students arrived on the island, they were happy to see the buildings completed and a new dining hall built.

The summer session moved along with much the same activities as the previous year. Unfortunately, Alexander Agassiz also became

The Anderson School of Natural History (above) 1874, (below) 1890
Photos: Marine Biological Laboratories

overworked and ill during the summer. At his doctor's advice, he left the island to recover. Professors Packard and Putnam, from the Peabody Academy of Science in Salem, took over the management of the school.[12] At the end of this summer session, the Anderson School of Natural History was once again considered a success.

When the school closed on August 29, few would have predicted it would never open again. Lack of funding made it impossible for the school to continue. Louis Agassiz had spent $47,000 of the original $50,000 during the first year. Consequently, the school had little money to open with in 1874, and the workboat *The Sprite* had to be sold. Anderson decided he could not support the school with his $10,000 endowment a year because the school no longer had the personality and prestige of Agassiz, or that of his son. Nevertheless, Anderson paid all the school's outstanding bills before he withdrew his support. Efforts to find other contributors proved to be fruitless.

Early in 1875, Alexander Agassiz officially notified Anderson that the school was permanently closed. It had been previously agreed upon by Anderson and Louis Agassiz that if the school should fail, ownership of the island would be given back to Anderson. By this time, Anderson and his wife had retired to Tarrytown, New York. While they were on vacation in Europe, John Anderson died in Paris on November 22, 1880.

The success of the Anderson School can be measured by the success of its students. Several became college presidents, many became college professors, and at least six developed their own laboratories. One of these laboratories is the Woods Hole Marine Biological Laboratory which was founded by C. O. Whitman and E. S. Minot. This laboratory acknowledges that it is a descendant of the Anderson School, and in 1923 a plaque was placed on a boulder at Penikese Island which reads:

In Commemoration
of the
Anderson School of Natural History
Established Fifty Years Ago on the Island of
Penikese by
Jean Louis Rodolphe Agassiz
Born 1807-Died 1873
The Marine Biological Laboratory
The Direct Descendant of the
Penikese School Erects This Tablet
1923

5
The Homer Turkey Farm
(1883-1905)

In 1883, George and Fred Homer, prominent businessmen in New Bedford, bought Penikese from Anderson's heirs,[1] then sold half of the island to William McGrorty. There was no division of land; the Homers and McGrorty each had half interest in the island. These three men turned Penikese into a large tenant turkey farm, and often went there to fish and to hunt ducks and geese.

The Homers did not spend much time on Penikese and left Flanders, the caretaker, in charge. In 1892, McGrorty sold his share of the island back to the Homers.[2] That same year the large building that was the Anderson School laboratory and dormitory burned. The cause of the fire was unknown.

There are no records of the subsequent caretakers after Flanders drowned in 1891. However, there is a fleeting reference to one in an article written by a college student named Linda C. L. Brannon. She and her college friends, some of whom were from Harvard and Radcliffe colleges, visited the island in 1893, perhaps as a pilgrimage to Agassiz. Brannon wrote "...our feet really touched the stones which the great scientist [Louis Agassiz] had trodden a little more than twenty years before."[3]

The caretaker that Brannon describes may not have enjoyed having the island invaded by a group of college students. In Brannon's article, she refers to the "watchman" as knowing nothing about the island and as never having heard of Agassiz!

When the group arrived at the house where "The Master" had lived, they were evidently taken to the portion of the house where the watchman lived with his dog. In Brannon's description she states "...at the back of the house were the 'Mess Rooms.' These were low and somewhat unattractive.* At the time they were occupied as living rooms by the watchman and his dumb companion, and we thought from their appearance that most of the housekeeping was left in charge of the dog." [4]

*This was probably the portion of the house built around 1794.

On July 18, 1905, George and Fred Homer were forced to sell their island to the Commonwealth of Massachusetts for $25,000, under the state's right of eminent domain. The Commonwealth needed a place to establish a hospital for its residents with leprosy, and Penikese—given its isolation—was considered an ideal location.

6
Leprosy (Hansen's Disease)

Leprosy has always been one of man's most dreaded diseases. Not only is it contagious and incurable, but carries with it the stigma of uncleanliness. When cases of leprosy appeared in the United States, the victims were sent to remote isolation centers immediately upon diagnosis. There they would spend the rest of their lives separated from their families and society. A victim's family suffered also. Often angry neighbors would do terrible things to the family, such as drive them from their home and then set the house on fire.

The following pages tell the story of how 36 people with leprosy lived on Penikese Island. The Penikese Island Leper Colony, also called the Penikese Island Hospital or Leprosarium, was open from November, 1905 until March, 1921. Many of the leprous people sent to Penikese had recently immigrated to the United States. Most of them were poor and several did not speak fluent English.* When Penikese closed in 1921, the patients were taken to a new, nation-wide facility in Carville, Louisiana. The United States Public Health Service Hospital in Carville is still in operation today. The following definition of Hansen's disease was edited by the staff at Carville:

> Hansen's disease (HD; leprosy) is an infectious disease caused by a bacterium (Mycobacterium leprae). Hansen's disease is contagious, but only about five percent of the world's population is not immune to it. Its incubation period can be quite long. Long-time association is not needed for someone to become infected. To be infected, one must come in contact with someone with the infectious form of the disease, and have some defect in one's immune system.
>
> There are three types of Hansen's disease of which a person can have either or a combination. In the lepromatous type (the more severe type), lesions may occur in any part of the body. It may include nodules and tubercules (red bumps). The eye is sometimes affected which can lead to blindness.

*The more affluent leprous residents of Massachusetts managed to avoid being sent to Penikese and were usually taken care of by their families in more pleasant settings.

The tuberculoid type is the least serious, but has no association with tuberculosis. The tuberculoid is called that because under the microscope, the pathology looks like tuberculosis. Lesions never appear in the lung. They are found in the skin and nerves.

The third type is borderline and it is a combination of the lepromatous and tuberculoid types.

In Hansen's disease, the bacterium affects mainly the cooler areas of the body (nose, hands and feet). The warmer areas are usually spared. In these areas, sometimes a condition called bone absorption occurs. This means that the body absorbs bone and cartilage that is in the nose, hands and feet, causing them to shrink to a small size. In the hands, the severe bone absorption is called "mitten hands." No part of the body falls off. What does occur often is that the loss of sensation may cause injuries and infections to go unnoticed, leading to deformities and mutilations.

It is estimated that there are 12 million cases of Hansen's disease around the world; about six thousand cases in the United States, and about 150 people with the disease at Carville.

Patients can now go unnoticed in public. They are treated in out-patient departments with the use of sulfone drugs along with others such as rifampin, clofazimine, or ethionamide. With this treatment, in almost all cases, the disease becomes inactivated and the patient is rendered non-contagious by the drugs, especially rifampin, in three or four days. Even after the patient is inactive, he or she can still have deformities that are permanent.

Most cases of Hansen's disease are found in tropical countries. In the United States, cases are primarily found in California, Florida, Hawaii, Louisiana, Texas and New York.

(Editor's Note: Today, the words "leper," "leprosy," and "leper colony" are no longer considered appropriate terms because of the social stigma often associated with the disease. The author has a deep regard for the victims of Hansen's disease and does not wish to show any disrespect by using these words. The words are used in this book simply because they were used during the time of which he writes.)

7
The Search for a
Leper Colony Site (1904-1905)

Louisiana was the first state to offer medical treatment for leprosy, but the Louisiana Leper Home, which opened in 1894, was only available to Louisiana residents. When several people in eastern Massachusetts were found to have leprosy in 1904, Massachusetts made plans to open a facility for its own leprous residents.

Before the Commonwealth bought Penikese Island from George and Fred Homer, state officials purchased an isolated 66-acre farm in Brewster on Cape Cod, known as the Bassett Farm on the north shore of Seymour's Pond.[1] The Massachusetts Board of Charity, the department then responsible for public health, purchased the land on December 31, 1904 for $1,550 from Franklin Underwood.*

When Cape residents, both year-round and summer, learned that they might have lepers as neighbors, they called for a public hearing. Railroad officials, land developers, and others interested in Cape Cod as a resort area flooded the State House with complaints. On January 8, 1905, a public hearing on the matter was held in Boston; it was the largest public hearing ever held in Massachusetts. There were so many protesters traveling from Cape Cod to Boston that railroad officials had to add on a special train. In the face of such opposition, the Board of Charity decided that Brewster, with about 750 residents, was too populated for a leper colony, and that a more secluded site was needed. Six months later, on June 6, 1905, the Board sold the Bassett Farm to the Town of Brewster for about $1,600.

The search for another site led state officials to inquire about the acquisition of Nashawena Island, one of the larger Elizabeth Islands. Their idea was to use one end of the island for the colony and the other end for a prison. When negotiations failed, the Board of Charity focused its attention on another Elizabeth Island, Penikese Island.

After the Commonwealth purchased Penikese from the Homers on July 18, 1905, complaints again poured into the State House. The coastal area of Buzzards Bay was being developed as a resort area

* Underwood had just bought the farm the day before from Greenleaf Bassett and his wife, for $50 less.

41

To the Residents of Buzzards Bay:

PETITION AND PROTEST

"Buzzards Bay Leper Colony"

HOW DO YOU LIKE THE SOUND?
HOW WILL IT AFFECT YOUR INTERESTS?

The purchase, July 12, 1905, by the State of the island of Penikese in Buzzards Bay to be used as a leper colony affects everyone having property interests on that Bay, however small and wherever located, and every effort should be made to avert the establishment of such an objectionable feature in your section.

Sentiment Rules the World

It may be that physically the proposition of establishing such an institution on the Bay does not intimately affect you personally; perhaps you may not have to ride in public conveyances with its inmates; probably there is no great danger from escaping lepers; but a little reflection will show that whenever the name of leper colony becomes associated with a place, that section no longer is considered desirable as a place of residence, and, as such, is a place avoided.

Probably the name "Gray Gables" and the fact of its being the residence of Grover Cleveland, together with the identification of the late lamented Joseph Jefferson with the Bay, have done more, outside of its natural advantages and attractions, to call attention to the Bay than any other one thing.

Can there be anything more repellent than to attach to the eighty miles or more of the water front of Buzzards Bay, the name of BUZZARDS BAY LEPER COLONY? You must be prepared, in case it is located there, to again and again answer the question

How near are you to the Leper Colony?

Ever bearing in mind that the stranger may not be as well informed as you as to localities and distances on the Bay.

NATIONAL LEPER COLONY

Senator W. Murray Crane has recently stated that at the next session of Congress an act would probably be passed establishing a National Leper Colony. Therefore, why should the expenditure of fifty thousand (50,000) dollars or more for a local leper colony of half a dozen lepers be imposed on Massachusetts. It will be a standing invitation to other states to dump their lepers here; *no laws can keep them out.*

Penikese petition and protest distributed in Massachusetts and Rhode Island

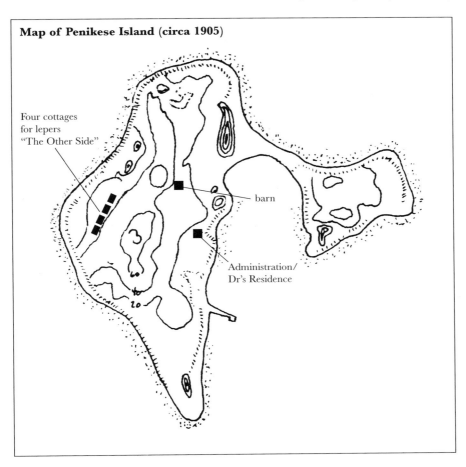

Map of Penikese Island (circa 1905)

Four cottages
for lepers
"The Other Side"

barn

Administration/
Dr's Residence

and land developers thought property values would drop if people had to look out at a leper colony. For months requests for a public hearing were made but, after their experience with the Brewster purchase, Governor Douglas and the Board of Charity refused to hold another hearing.

Soon the Board of Charity drew up plans to convert Penikese into a leper colony. For four months the island was full of activity, as it had been when the Anderson School was being built. On the east side of the island, the Anderson's house and barn were repaired, as well as small buildings the Homers had used. On the west side, which later became known as "the other side," four one-story cottages were built—each measuring 27 feet wide and 36 feet long. They were designed for two patients and included a kitchen, bath, living room,

Leper cottages and hospital, 1925
Photo: Winthrop Packard, U.S. Dept. Fish and Wildlife

Foundation of hospital and leper cottages, 1979
Photo: by author

44

porch, and two bedrooms.[2]

On the top of Penikese's highest hill, which is 82 feet above sea level, a 10,000-gallon reservoir was dug and lined with brick. Fresh water was then pumped from a well that was dug below the hill to the reservoir and then sent through gravity-fed pipes to the cottages and other buildings.

The Board of Charity located five people who were willing to work on the island. They were: a superintendent who would receive $2,000 a year; a farmer-boatman,* a housekeeper, and a female attendant who each would receive $600 a year; and a male attendant who would receive $1.00 a day.

On October 15, 1905, Dr. Louis Edmonds of Harwich was placed on the state payroll as the Superintendent of the Penikese Island Hospital. Edmonds, a native of England, had studied medicine at Harvard and worked in a hospital in Worcester, before moving to Harwich where he had practiced general medicine for 11 years.[3] He qualified for the position because he had successfully diagnosed a man with leprosy the year before.

---

*It was hoped that farming the island would help feed and clothe the patients and staff.

8
Penikese Island
Leper Colony Opens (1905-1906)

The Commonwealth of Massachusetts opened the Penikese Island Leper Colony without ceremony on November 18, 1905.* All Massachusetts residents with leprosy were now legally required to live on the island. On that cold, damp November day five leprous people arrived in Fairhaven. They were accompanied by the colony's new superintendent Dr. Lewis Edmonds, his assistant Ceasar Monteriro and the island's new caretakers—Josiah Young and his wife, Grace. All of the staff were from Harwich.

There were also several doctors in attendance from various local and state health departments. The patients—four men and a woman—had to wait in the train for three to four hours for the weather to improve before they could board a boat to cross Buzzards Bay to Penikese. The patients were: Frank Pina, Goon Lee Dip, John Roderick, Yee Toy, and Isabelle Barros.

Dip, Roderick, and Toy had come from Gallops Island in Boston Harbor, where there was a temporary shelter for lepers.** Pina had arrived from his home in Harwich, and Barros arrived from her home in Wareham.

Dr. Edmonds made a report on each patient when they arrived. These reports contained information, such as the patient's age, place of birth, marital status, physical condition, and character traits. While the colony was in operation, a progress report was submitted each year to the Board of Charity, describing the conditions of the patients.***

Frank Pina, 38, was a native of the Cape Verde Islands and the man that Dr. Edmonds had diagnosed. Before arriving on Penikese, Pina had been cared for at his cottage in Harwich, while his wife and eight children were required by health officials to leave their home and live in another part of town. When Pina left Harwich, these offi-

*It was supposed to open November 17, but a storm delayed it one day.
**The city of Boston had facilities on Gallops Island where they placed people with contagious diseases. Hospitals refused to accept leprosy cases so the Board of Charity used these facilities for leprous patients.
***For more information on each patient, see *Reported Cases of Leprosy in Massachusetts* in the Appendix.

cials guaranteed the town that they would destroy the cottage and reimburse the owner at the assessed rate. This was done, it was thought at the time, to prevent the spread of the disease.

Goon Lee Dip, 23, was Chinese. Over time he was known on the island as "Willie Goon" or "The Chinaman." Dip reported that he was born in the United States and went to China to be married.* In 1902, he left his wife and son in China and returned to the United States. He lived two years in Roxbury, where he worked in a laundry. On June 6, 1904, he was diagnosed with leprosy and sent to Gallops Island. When Dip arrived at Penikese, Dr. Edmonds described him as "able-bodied, content and willing to work." He later became very popular with the other patients and staff, and was described as "cheerful even under the most trying conditions."

John Roderick, 34, was an unmarried Portuguese sailor who was diagnosed with leprosy on August 14, 1904. He spent one week on Gallops Island and then escaped. Five months later he appeared at the Chelsea Marine Hospital, where he was again diagnosed with leprosy and again sent to Gallops Island. When this man arrived on Penikese, Dr. Edmonds described him as "very sick and slowly dying."

Yee Toy, 25, was Chinese and had spent four years in Newburyport, where he had worked in a laundry. On January 18, 1905, he was diagnosed as leprous and sent to Gallops Island, where he stayed until he was sent to Penikese. Dr. Edmonds described Toy as "a spirited, courageous person who liked to keep busy."

Isabelle Barros, 27, was the only female patient to arrive on Opening Day. She was also an immigrant from the Cape Verde Islands. Mrs. Barros was diagnosed earlier that year on April 24, 1905, but was allowed to remain isolated in her Wareham home until the Penikese Colony opened. Her husband, Napoleon Barros, acted as her nurse while their two small children (a boy and a girl) were placed in a foster home and became wards of the state. Mrs. Barros told Edmonds that she once had smallpox and malaria and suspected her father of having leprosy. When she arrived on the island, Mrs. Barros was described as "weak, anemic, and debilitated." There was no mention of her being four months pregnant. She remained the only female patient for two years.

Once on the island, the patients were taken to the west side, or

*It was not uncommon for immigrants to claim that they had been born in the United States in order to secure citizenship.

"other side," of the island in a new horse drawn cart. Here, they found their cottages neat and well-furnished, and in some cases better than what they were used to. Pina shared a cottage with Roderick, whom he had known in the Cape Verde Islands. Dip shared a cottage with Toy, and Mrs. Barros shared a cottage with the female attendant.[1]

Committed to the loneliness of an island, their bodies full of pain and fever, separated from their families, and deprived of their freedom, the lepers became hermits. If approached by a visitor or staff person, they would run and hide. They also became childish and spiteful—refusing to eat, wasting supplies yet demanding more.[2]

In contrast, the general public was now pleased with the decision to establish the Penikese Colony. However, the residents of the other Elizabeth Islands and most of the nearby mainlanders still feared infection from the disease. Problems arose when local boatmen would not approach the island with needed supplies. High prices were paid to ensure delivery. Staff members who went to the mainland for supplies were often shunned by wharf men and merchants. The fear of this disease led the local citizens to ridiculous behavior, such as holding handkerchiefs to their faces as they passed by the island and threatening their misbehaving children with bogeymen stories about lepers.[3]

As the patients on Penikese began to accept their fate, relations between them improved. By the spring of 1906, lifelong friendships had begun. John Roderick's condition was stabilized, and Frank Pina's health had greatly improved. Goon Lee Dip and Yee Toy were helping Pina maintain the buildings.

On March 8, 1906, Isabelle Barros gave birth to a healthy baby boy. What a joy this baby must have been to the exiles![4] After 20 days, however, the baby was removed from the island; Mrs. Barros knew she couldn't keep him for fear he may contract leprosy. Wisely, she named the baby Leontine Lincoln Barros, after the chairman of the Board of Charity, Leontine Lincoln. Chairman Lincoln was in charge of children who had become wards of the Commonwealth.

Even more excitement came six months later when Dr. Edmonds announced that he had cured Mrs. Barros of leprosy, and that she would be going home. Newspapers throughout the state reported on the great work of Dr. Edmonds.

Mrs. Barros' family and friends were anxious for her release. Dr. Edmonds, however, had failed to notify the Board of Charity of his plans to release her. When the board learned of his intent, they sent doctors to the island to examine Mrs. Barros. These doctors found that Dr. Edmonds had erred in his diagnosis, and that Mrs. Barros was not cured.[5] Soon after this event, Dr. Edmonds resigned and opened a private practice in Roxbury. Mrs. Barros remained on Penikese.

The Commonwealth now had three Barros children that no one wanted. For the next ten years, the children bounced in and out of several foster homes. Finally, they were taken in by Joseph and Josephine Alves of New Bedford, who later had six children of their own. Here they remained for the rest of their childhoods.

Leontine Barros, who preferred to be called Leo, attended parochial schools in New Bedford, and in 1931 he moved to Medford where he spent most of his adult life. Barros served in World War II as a member of the Air Force, and in 1947, he joined the staff of the Don Bosco Technical High School in Boston where he taught woodworking, English, and history. At night, Barros attended classes at Boston University where he received a Bachelor's Degree in English. After 30 years, he retired from Don Bosco, and worked as a substitute teacher in Medford.

Leo Barros was married four times, raised two sons, and was always active in his church, community, and with local youth programs. The City of Medford twice awarded him a *Key to the City* for his work with local youth.

He died at the age of 91 on May 10, 1996.[6]

9
The New Superintendent, Dr. Frank H. Parker (1907)

Dr. Frank H. Parker became Superintendent of the Penikese Island Hospital on January 1, 1907, and spent the next 15 years treating lepers there.

Dr. Parker had practiced general medicine in Malden for 22 years and had an interest in smallpox and leprosy. He was born in Portland, Maine on July 4, 1855. His father, a sea captain, died two years later while on a trip to China. Soon after his death, the family moved to East Boston where Frank spent his youth and received his education. He studied at the Boston Grammar School, the Boston English High School, and at Boston's College of Physicians and Surgeons, which is now Tufts University. In 1885, he married Marion E. King and the couple moved to Malden where he opened his practice.

Mrs. Parker was born in Castine, Maine on October 8, 1857. The family later moved to East Boston where she met Frank Parker. After their marriage, she became prominent in social and charitable circles and was a freelance writer, who published under her maiden name.

The couple had two sons, Howard K. born in 1886 and Ralph R. born in 1888. On December 27, 1906, Mrs. Parker accompanied her husband to Penikese and there became a valuable aid to him and was loved by the lepers.

When the Parkers' friends and associates heard they were planning to work on Penikese for a year, many of them feared the Parkers would catch the disease, as the martyred Father Damien* had at the Molokai Leper Colony in Hawaii. The Parkers scoffed at the idea of becoming martyrs and willingly gave up their busy life to care for the lepers on Penikese.** [1]

Dr. and Mrs. Parker were so enthusiastic about their new work that they arrived on the island five days early. This enthusiasm and spirit were appreciated by both the patients and the Board of Charity. That year the Board successfully pressured legislators to make more

*Damien (1840-1889) was a Belgian Roman Catholic missionary who supervised the Molokai Colony for over 25 years and contracted the disease.
**The Parkers later extended their stay on the island to 15 years, until the colony closed in 1921.

Some of the Lepers on Penikese, Left to Right—Lucy Peterson, Goon Lee Dep, Mrs. Barros.

Lucy Peterson, Goon Lee Dip and Isabelle Barros as they appeared in a newspaper story *Source: Harvard's Francis A. Countway Library of Medicine in Boston*

money available to the colony. It was used to build a cottage and stone fences, and to increase livestock.

Dr. Parker was a kind, easy-natured man who had a genuine interest in each of his patients. He often went to great lengths to make their lives more comfortable. If certain items they wanted were not in the state warehouses, he ordered them from the manufacturer.[2] Many times he used his own money to pay for these items.

Mrs. Parker was also kind-hearted. She arranged to get radios, record players, books, and magazines for the patients. These mainland pleasures helped mitigate the pain of leprosy and social ostracism. At first, when there were no clergymen available, she held religious services for the patients.

Dr. Parker realized that his patients' self-respect often suffered. One of the first things he did when he arrived was lift the ban that restricted the patients to the three acres near their cottages. With the ban lifted, they could go anywhere on the island except near the

Administration Building, where they might frighten a visitor or delivery person. Parker encouraged his patients to take care of each other whenever possible and gave them jobs at which they could earn small wages. With this money, they could order personal items from the New Bedford stores.

Under Dr. Parker's care, the patients' general health improved after a few months. Parker attributed this not only to his medications, but to good food, fresh air, and sunshine. To encourage his patients to spend more time outdoors, Parker suggested they raise small vegetable and flower gardens. They liked this idea and soon there was competition among them to see who could grow the best garden. Some of these gardens must have been quite successful, as today there are still a few daffodils and irises growing alongside the cottages' foundations.

During the Parkers' first year, five new patients came to live on the island. On May 31, 1907, Charles W. Beals and Joseph Needham arrived. Beals, 54, was from Hyde Park and had lived in Massachusetts for 18 years. He was suspected of being leprous on October 29, 1906, and held for seven months on Gallops Island for tests. Beals told Parker that he might have contracted the disease from handling foreign money as an accountant for an express company. He also said that he had never left the country. Joseph Needham, 23, was from Trinidad, West Indies, and had lived in Somerville only a short time before being sent to Penikese. Dr. Parker considered his case to be in its advanced stage.* Beals and Needham were most likely assigned to the fourth cottage, which up to this point had been occupied by the male attendant.

Lucy Peterson, 27, was the second woman to be admitted to the island hospital. She arrived on July 24, two days after she was diagnosed with leprosy. Miss Peterson, an immigrant from Russia, had been living and working in Brookline for four years as a domestic. When she arrived on Penikese Island, she was described as "pretty and well-formed." It was also reported that her disease was in its early stage.

Miss Peterson proved herself to be a very capable woman and a great asset to the colony. She cleaned the cottages of the patients who had become incapacitated and acted as nurse and interpreter. For her work, she received $2.00 a week. Isabelle Barros and she became

---

*It is unclear why this man was not deported to his home in the West Indies since he had not lived in the United States long enough to acquire citizenship.

Penikese Island Cemetery, 1925 *Photo: U.S. Dept. Fish and Wildlife*

close friends and before long they moved into a new cottage called the Women's Cottage. This cottage was erected on the south side of the island, about 500 yards from the others.[3]

On June 21, John Roderick died, after spending 19 months on the island. He was the man Edmonds had described as "slowly dying." Dr. Parker reported that his death was caused from a complication of diseases. Roderick was buried on the north side of the island, which later became the Island Cemetery.*

On August 29, another Russian immigrant, Morris Goldblatt, 41, came to live on Penikese. When Dr. Parker examined Goldblatt, he found the leprosy to be in its advanced stages. Goldblatt had large ulcers on one arm and partial loss of sensation in both arms and on his nose. Before moving to East Boston, where he was diagnosed, Goldblatt had lived in Lynn with his wife and five children and had worked in a leather factory.

One problem that continually plagued the island residents was the lack of fresh water. During that summer, fresh water had to be rationed and baths were taken in salt water. To prevent this from happening again, a 100,000-gallon reservoir was put in next to the smaller one. It was thought that with a daily use of about 250 gallons, these two reservoirs could supply the island during any drought.[4]

---

*For more information, see *The Penikese Island Cemetery* in the Appendix.

On December 3, Bertha Osis, 19, was the fifth new patient admitted to the island hospital that year. She had immigrated to the states from Russia in 1905 and had worked in Brookline. She was described as beautiful. Her only sign of leprosy was a small spot on her cheek. She had gone to see a doctor to find out why a small blemish would not heal, and 24 hours later found herself in a leper colony! Because she had not lived in the United States long enough to acquire citizenship, she was detained on Penikese to determine if her diagnosis was correct.

In Parker's annual report, he stated that the health of the patients had improved. He even described Isabelle Barros as a "healthy-looking specimen of humanity."[5] The patients living on the island at this time were Frank Pina, Goon Dip, Yee Toy, Isabelle Barros, Charles Beals, Joseph Needham, Lucy Peterson, Morris Goldblatt, and Bertha Osis.

The farmer-boatman, whom state health officials had hired when the colony was established, must have had a busy year in 1907. He reported harvesting three tons of hay, two tons of corn fodder, a ton of pumpkins, 100 bushels of turnips, 40 bushels of carrots, and many bushels of squash, potatoes, beets and cabbage. This was a considerable crop for only the second year. Besides farming 65 of the island's 75 acres, the farmer tended the livestock and operated the island's boat.[6]

10
Improved Facilities (1908-1909)

During a winter storm, the island's motor boat *Keepsake* was washed up on the beach and wrecked. Dr. Parker did not seem particularly upset about the loss, as he recorded that he needed a new boat that was "dependable." *Keepsake's* engine was known for breaking down, once with a boat full of health officials. The state purchased for island use a 28-foot auxiliary catboat.[1]

In 1908, a one-story building was erected on the foundation of the old Anderson School dining hall, and was used as a carpenters' shop and a storage area. It also housed extra workmen from the mainland who might be hired occasionally.[2]

Workmen no doubt used this building when they built a new 200-foot wharf and stone pier. Adequate dockage had always been a problem and this new addition made it possible for larger boats, such as coal barges, to dock. Before this, the coal needed for heat and cooking had to be brought near the island on large barges, loaded offshore into smaller boats, and then brought ashore.[3] The lower price of coal delivery soon offset the $5,000 wharf and pier cost.*

In keeping with the idea that the farm should help the islanders become as self-sufficient as possible, the livestock was increased to 3 cows, 2 heifers, 1 bull, 1 horse, 15 pigs, and over 300 hens. A sheep shed was also built to protect the farm's 85 sheep.

On May 10, 1908, Bertha Osis was deported, after her condition had been confirmed. She left reluctantly because she felt that if anyone could heal her, Dr. Parker could. Miss Osis was from Courland, Russia, near Lucy Peterson's family. Before leaving, she promised Miss Peterson that she would visit her mother and sisters. Miss Osis was taken to New Bedford and placed on the freighter *Ramona,* which sailed her to New York. On her trip she was required to stay downwind of the crew, and if she failed to do so, the crew would yell, "Leper!" In New York Harbor, people in tugs and small private crafts

---

*In 1909, it was learned that the channel to the new wharf and pier was not deep enough for coal barges and that dredging would cost $15,000.

59

circled the ship to catch a glimpse of the girl. Miss Osis was then transferred to the steamer *Hellig Olav* and taken back to Russia.[4]

It was no coincidence that the *Hellig Olav* was the same ship that brought Miss Osis to the United States. It was common for authorities to deport lepers on the same ships they had immigrated on.[5] By doing this, they hoped that ship owners would be more careful about the people they brought to the United States. Ships leaving the country with a leper on board would have very unprofitable voyages. Passengers would cancel their trip, dock hands would not load or unload freight, and often the crew would quit.

Most of the patients at this time were in good health. Goon Lee Dip and Yee Toy had cut off their queues* as a expression of good feelings toward the United States and the treatment they were receiving. Dip was sporting a mustache much like the style of Dr. Parker's. Frank Pina and Joseph Needham, though, were suffering from eye problems, which were common symptoms of advanced leprosy. Dr. Parker sent for an eye specialist but little was known about how to cope with the disease once it reached this stage.

In 1909, several more improvements were made. An employee dining hall was added to the Administration Building. Repairs were made to the workmen's quarters, a vegetable cellar was constructed, and a new flag pole was put up. Dr. Parker also installed a 240-foot marine railway which he used to haul his new catboat out of the water in case of a storm.[6]

*Commonly called a pigtail.

Archie Thomas (above) and Emma Thomas (below) as they appeared in a newspaper story *Source: Harvard's Francis A. Countway Library of Medicine in Boston*

11
Penikese's
Youngest Patient (1909)

Four new patients arrived on Penikese in 1909, joining the eight others. Among them was Penikese's youngest patient, Archibald James B. Thomas, 16, who arrived on March 27, 1909.

Archie, as he was known, had immigrated from Barbados, West Indies with his mother when he was nine. They had lived in Upton, where Mrs. Thomas was a supervisor in a hat factory while Archie attended the local school. Archie was a good student and interested in physics, electricity, and wireless telegraphy. When Archie developed a rash, Mrs. Thomas took him to a Boston hospital where he was diagnosed with leprosy. He was isolated for five days while doctors agonized over what to do with him. Finally, they realized that legally there was no choice but to send him to Penikese.

After the initial shock of her son's diagnosis, Mrs. Thomas decided to join her son on Penikese so she could take care of him. In order to do this, she needed permission from the Board of Charity. The Board, however, was very reluctant to let Mrs. Thomas go because they feared she would contract the disease. So, Mrs. Thomas quit her job, sold her possessions, and moved to a friend's house in Somerville, where she would be nearer to Boston and the Board of Charity. By this time, newspapers were carrying full-page articles about Mrs. Thomas' plight complete with pictures of Archie, Mrs. Thomas, their home, and Archie's school friends. This publicity helped the Board of Charity decide to allow Mrs. Thomas to go.

After waiting many weeks for this decision, Mrs. Thomas was quoted as saying, "My husband is dead, I haven't a chick nor a child with the exception of Archie. There is no one else who needs me as he does. There is no one else to whom I owe my devotion…Don't pity me, be glad, as I am, that I can go."[1]

When Mrs. Thomas first arrived at Penikese, she lived with her son in his cottage and had the same restrictions as the patients. Later she was given a position as Nurse's Assistant at a token salary of $200 a year.[2] In this position, she had complete freedom of the

Solomon Goodman, as he appeared in a newspaper story
Source: Harvard's Francis A. Countway Library of Medicine in Boston

island and could visit the mainland whenever she pleased.

Soloman Goodman, 64, arrived on Penikese the same day Archie did. He was a Russian immigrant and had lived in Boston's North End, where he had taught Hebrew to children. For three years he had trouble walking and was treated for fallen arches. When his problem was found to be caused by leprosy, he was sent to Penikese.

The next patient to arrive was Demetrias Phresa, a 25-year-old Greek man, who had been employed in Haverhill as a cook. Phresa's case had first been diagnosed as impetigo, a contagious skin disease; while he was a patient at the state infirmary in Tewksbury, doctors diagnosed his illness as leprosy. He arrived on Penikese the same day that he was diagnosed, April 24, 1909. While on the island, Phresa caused discipline problems. He was short-tempered and once, during an argument, wounded another patient with a knife. This was the only reported act of violence in the colony.[3] Everyone must have been relieved when this man left the island later that year. Like Bertha Osis, Phresa had not been in the country long enough to acquire citizenship and was deported on October 15, 1909.

When health officials arrived to send Phresa to New York, he refused to leave and had to be restrained. Understanding little English, Phresa thought he was being returned to Greece to be tried for murder. He continued to be restrained aboard the schooner *Andrew G. Pierce* and eventually became raving mad. The schooner was caught in a storm, and had to be towed into New York Harbor. Phresa was then placed on the steamer *Argentina* and deported to Greece. The health officer who accompanied him to New York was later interviewed by a newspaper reporter and quoted as saying, "I want to forget it, and I will never talk of it to any living man, for it is an incident that I wish to consider dead to me."[4]

It was not uncommon for lepers to deny that they had leprosy. Mary Martinez, the next patient to arrive on the island, was one such case. Mrs. Martin, as she was later known, was a 44-year-old widow from the Cape Verde Islands. She had lived in New Bedford with her married daughter and was employed as a cook. On December 14, she was diagnosed as having leprosy and would have immediately gone to Penikese, if a storm had not closed the New Bedford seaport for three days. During this time, Mrs. Martinez was quarantined in her home with a police guard. After she left, her home was fumigated with special gases before her daughter was allowed to return. When a home was fumigated, doors and windows were sealed and all closets and dressers were opened. Then a heated chemical such as sulfur or formaldehyde was released, permeating everything and leaving the home germ-free.

There were 11 patients on Penikese at Christmas time that year, and many gifts were sent to the island. One gift was a telegraph set for Archie from the New Bedford Women's Society.[5] With this set Archie was able to receive messages from his school friends in Upton. He was unable to send messages that far away, so instead responded by mail.

12
A New Hospital
Building (1910-1911)

In the summer and fall of 1910, a hospital building was constructed by the Z. B. Davis Corporation of New Bedford. This two-story
wooden structure was built between two cottages, connecting them so
that the complex measured 45 feet by 70 feet. Attached to the back
was an ell that measured 30 feet by 30 feet.[1] This new hospital contained bedrooms for the sicker patients and treatment rooms, as well
as a reading room, amusement room, kitchen, and dining hall. There
were also living quarters for a full-time nurse. Soon after the comple-
tion of this building, the Women's Universalist Society of New
Bedford contributed money for a billiard table to be put in the amusement room.

It wasn't long before the new building became the center of activity for the patients, a place to socialize. Hospital patients ate in the
new building, and those in the cottages ate in their homes. The cooks
often took care to prepare vegetables the patients had raised in their
gardens, as well as fish they had caught. Mrs. Parker sometimes
served the patients afternoon tea, and once a week she and her husband joined them for a dinner party.

In the fall of 1910, there was once again a lack of fresh water.
This time the shortage, which was caused by drought, was so severe
that water had to be shipped to the island from New Bedford. This
cost the state $600. Over $1,000 had already been spent that summer
digging wells, which turned up only brackish water.[2]

On December 13, 1910, Marion Parker was appointed postmaster of the Penikese Island Post Office.[3] Mrs. Parker wanted a post
office on the island so she could be assured of regular delivery, instead
of depending upon the whims of local boatmen. The salary she
received as postmaster was the only income that Mrs. Parker ever
received for her work on the island. It was part of her job to fumigate
the patients' mail. She used a Listers Formaldehyde Fumigator. First
she would cut off the corners of the letters, then place them in a box
that was arranged so the fumes from burning a formaldehyde candle

would enter, thus making the letters germ-free.[4]

In addition to his work on Penikese, Dr. Parker was appointed as a County Medical Examiner. Because he was the only physician on the Elizabeth Islands, he was sometimes called upon to tend to the sick and dying on the neighboring islands. When he was on the mainland, he was asked occasionally to diagnose suspected cases of leprosy.

Two new patients arrived on Penikese in 1911, Iwa Umezakia on January 26, and Flavia Ballentino on May 15. Umezakia, 26, was a Japanese carpenter and cabinet maker from Boston's South End. He was described as being of considerable intelligence, yet antisocial. Umezakia was very unhappy on Penikese and brooded over the Japanese government's refusal to allow his return to Japan.

Mrs. Ballentino, 47, immigrated from Italy and was living in Boston's North End. When she developed a rash, it was first diagnosed as smallpox. Mrs. Ballentino was then isolated at Massachusetts General Hospital, where tests showed her disease to be leprosy. She found it very difficult to adjust to the isolation on Penikese.

In 1911, Penikese Island Hospital was valued at $81,877.64 and the operating budget was a little less than $12,000 a year. This brought the weekly cost of each patient to $18.29. All of these expenses were paid for by the taxpayers of the Commonwealth.[5] Both Dr. Parker and the Board of Charity thought that much of the taxpayers' money was wasted because they believed the patients could be treated on the mainland like others with contagious diseases.

13
Fire! (1912)

On the morning of January 13, 1912, the Administration Building caught fire. Archie Thomas sent a telegraph message to a ship passing by Penikese and the message was relayed to New Bedford, where the revenue cutter *Achusnet* and its crew were dispatched to aid the islanders. In the meantime, a red distress flag was raised on the island. People on Cuttyhunk noticed the distress signal and sent the tugboat *John T. Sherman* with the crew of the Cuttyhunk Life Saving Service to help fight the fire. Unfortunately, the Administration Building was completely destroyed. This building had been the Anderson-Agassiz home and was now the Parkers' home. It had also housed the colony's offices. Lost in the fire were all of the patients' records, Dr. Parker's library, and most of the Parkers' personal property. Residents of Cuttyhunk and New Bedford put aside their fears and rushed to offer food, blankets, and clothing, but the offers were politely declined as few of these types of items were damaged. It was later discovered that the fire was caused by a faulty chimney.* [1]

While the new Administration Building was being built, Dr. and Mrs. Parker moved into the Hospital Building on "the other side" of the island. It was decided that future structures, including the new Administration Building, would be built of concrete instead wood.

The new Administration Building was constructed on almost the same spot as the old had been. The building cost a little under $30,000. It contained the colony's offices, the Parkers' residence, the Post Office, some of the staff's quarters, a kitchen, and a dining room. This two-story building measured 46 feet by 62 feet. Attached to it were two one-story ells. The ell on the east side measured 20 feet by 26 feet and was Dr. Parker's laboratory. The west ell measured 20 feet by 40 feet and housed an electric power plant. At this time, electricity was installed in the new Administration Building as well as the patients' cottages and the Hospital Building. Later, a refrigeration plant was built and, for the first time, the islanders could make their own ice.[2]

*It had always been a concern that one of the patients whose hands were numb from leprosy might drop a kerosene lamp and start a fire, but this was not the case.

Four new patients were admitted to Penikese in 1912 to join the other 13 patients on the island. Elais Applebaum, 55, arrived on May 11. This man had immigrated from Russia and had lived in Boston's South End and in Roxbury. Henry Chin Yen, 30, arrived on June 15. He had lived in China with his wife and son before immigrating to the United States. Yen was in Boston only two days before being diagnosed as leprous. Marion J. Braga, 34, was from the Azores and had lived in the New Bedford Almshouse where he acted as a fireman. He was sent to Penikese on June 28, but because he was not a citizen of the United States, he was deported on August 13.

While waiting for a ship to leave New Bedford for the Cape Verde Islands, Manuiel Coriea Baptiste was apprehended by health officials and found to be leprous. Baptiste, 24, was planning to return to his homeland to be married. He was sent to Penikese on November 10.

Every day the Parkers witnessed the agony of their patients, which deepened their desire to find a cure for leprosy. Dr. Parker consulted with leprosy experts from all over the world and conducted experiments in his own laboratory, but was unsuccessful. Several times he thought he had cured a patient but each time the disease would slowly reappear. Parker never gave up hope and his optimism encouraged his patients.

One of the patients who had been sustained by this hope was Charles Beals, who died on November 7, 1912. Beals' body was taken to Boston for burial. He was the only patient who was taken off the island for interment.

The effect of leprosy was slowly taking its toll on the earlier patients. Frank Pina was still having trouble with his eyes. Goon Lee Dip and Solomon Goodman were having trouble with their feet, and Lucy Peterson complained of nose and throat problems. But Joseph Needham, who was near death, made a recovery from pneumonia. At the end of 1912, there were 15 patients on the island: 11 men and four women.

14
A New Image (1912-1914)

With its up-to-date Hospital and new Administration Building and laboratory, Penikese experienced many changes during the year 1912. The Board of Charity felt that the public would never allow lepers to be treated on the mainland, so they decided that Penikese should become a permanent undertaking of the Commonwealth. They believed that Penikese should be regarded as a hospital for the treatment of lepers, rather than an isolated leper colony. With this in mind, a Supervisory Board was established for Penikese, a full-time resident nurse was hired, and specialists and students were invited to study on the island. Dr. Parker was also given an assistant, Dr. James A. Honeij.[1]

Dr. Honeij, a graduate of Tufts College and a physician at Boston City Hospital, was elected as Dr. Parker's assistant by the Medical Review Committee. It was also arranged by the Board of Charity and Harvard University that Parker and Honeij would have available to them all the facilities at the Harvard Medical School.[2] With the equipment on the island and the facilities at Harvard, Penikese Island Hospital was now the world's best-equipped leprosarium.

In 1913, there were two new patients, one death, one attempted escape, and one release. One of the new patients was Wong Quong, who arrived on March 13 from Boston's Chinatown, where he worked as a waiter and cook. Dr. Parker described his condition as "well-advanced."

Elais Applebaum's case was also "well-advanced" but after ten months on the island, his family arranged to have him released. There is no record of how this was arranged or where Applebaum went. The only reference made to this event was in the 1913 annual report which stated he was "released for treatment elsewhere." This may have been a situation where a middle-to-upper class family applied enough political pressure and had the financial means to place Applebaum in a more pleasant environment. The public was not notified of the release until many months later.[3]

Joseph Needham died on August 8, 1913, after being a patient for six years. He had requested a Catholic priest to attend his burial but, at this time, there was no chaplain assigned to the island. Nevertheless, his wishes were honored and a priest was located on the mainland. He arrived late in the evening, and Needham was buried that night in the Island Cemetery.[4] (The only other patient buried on the island at this time was John Roderick.)

Iwa Umezakia, the unhappy Japanese patient, made an escape on September 18, by rowing a boat 14 miles to Padanaram in Massachusetts. From there he took a trolley to New Bedford and then a train to Boston. That day Umezakia roamed around Boston for several hours and then went to the Detention Hospital where he asked to be cured, or sent back to Japan to die among his family. Instead, he was returned to Penikese where he spent the rest of his life. When his escape became known, the trolley he rode was removed from the line and fumigated. This took some time and many people in New Bedford had to walk home from work that night.[5]

The other new patient in 1913 was Hyman Klein, 26, a Jewish immigrant and brush maker from Boston. When he arrived on November 12, his leprosy was described as the tubercular form and he had a number of ulcers on his throat and nose.*

Christmas that year was celebrated in the Hospital amusement room. Music was played on a new organ and a Christmas tree was surrounded by gifts. Mrs. Parker had gone to Boston to get her gifts for the patients and to buy presents that the patients wished to give each other. Many other gift packages arrived from all over the country. Mrs. Parker held a religious service. Then hymns and carols were sung and a Christmas dinner served.[6]

In his year-end report, Dr. Honeij described the conditions of some of the patients in the following way. He stated that Soloman Goodman was rarely depressed and had a "rugged constitution." Yee Toy had a history of "fits" and also of gonorrhea, and was losing sensation in his right leg. Mary Martin had developed claw-like hands. Lucy Peterson's nose had flattened and it had the appearance of a

---

*Klein later wrote an interesting tale about a shipwrecked sailor who came to his cottage one night. Klein was up late reading when at about 2:00 a.m. there was a knock on his cottage door. Expecting it to be another patient, Klein called "come in" and in walked a stranger. After introducing himself, the stranger explained that he was from a schooner that was grounded offshore of the island. The sailor had noticed Klein's light and rowed ashore to get help. The stranger asked Klein what kind of place the island was. Unfortunately, the reactions of the sailor were not described, but the schooner was gone the next day.

lion's nose. Umezakia had developed active signs of syphilis and Mrs. Ballentino was going insane. Dr. Parker tried to get her released, insisting she would not endanger anyone.[7]

In contrast, Henry Chin Yen was responding well to treatment and showed little evidence of the disease. Hence, Yen appealed to the Board of Charity to be allowed to return to his home in China. Parker and Honeij supported Yen's appeal and felt that his traveling across the country would not endanger the public. The Board agreed and made transportation arrangements for Yen to be released on January 3, 1914. The public was not informed of his release until two weeks later[8] because an earlier announcement would have threatened Yen's safety. If it had been known that Yen was traveling across the country, he could have been removed from a train and set upon by mobs.

15
The Island Chaplain
(1914)

The Parkers felt that the religious services offered on Penikese were not meeting the spiritual needs of the patients. An appeal was made to the New Bedford Ministerial Union for a chaplain to be sent to the island each Sunday, but most local clergymen were either too busy in their own churches or concerned about getting seasick on the trip to the island. Finally, the Ministerial Union assigned one chaplain, who was to represent all religions.[1]

Reverend Nathan Bailey, from the North Baptist Church in New Bedford, was appointed to this position in 1914[2], and quickly realized he could not hold a regular church service because most patients understood little English. In time, he discovered that the patients liked to sing, so in each service he incorporated a lot of hymn singing and short readings from the Bible. Reverend Bailey also encouraged patients by giving them individual attention. Soon he became their great friend and confidant.

Reverend Bailey was not paid for his work. He considered it a privilege to represent the Ministerial Union and to give service to the lepers. He was the colony's only chaplain and held that position until the island colony closed in 1921. All patients were encouraged to take part in the religious services for many reasons, least of which was to distract them from their disease.

For further distractions, they were encouraged to pursue their many interests. Some of the patients wanted pets, but the Board of Charity feared that leprosy might be spread to the animals.* For some reason this rule did not apply to birds, and Isabelle Barros and Iwa Umezakia kept birds as pets. Mrs. Barros had a green and yellow parrot named "Lolita," which she left to Umezakia when she died. Umezakia had a crow and a bittern both of which he had caught and trained. The crow reportedly could talk in Japanese and the bittern, which was caught as a young bird, followed Umezakia on his walks around the island.[3]

*It was later found that animals could not catch or spread leprosy, but at this time every precaution was taken to prevent the spread of the disease.

Laundry building, 1925 *Photo: U.S. Dept. Fish and Wildlife*

By this time Isabelle Barros and Lucy Peterson had moved to rooms in the Hospital Building and Umezakia moved to the Women's Cottage, because he preferred to live alone. In one room he had a shrine with an ebony Buddha. Umezakia also kept a garden by the back door of his cottage. Some of his daffodils still bloom today! Also growing near the site of this cottage is a peculiar strain of blackberries. This strain has been found in only two other places—Concord, Massachusetts and southern New Hampshire. Someone may have sent cuttings of the unusual bush to Umezakia.

The only new construction that took place in 1914 was the building of a new laundry.[4] This small unit was built of concrete and most of its walls are still standing today. Goon Lee Dip was in charge of the laundry and Yee Toy helped him. It is not known what salary Toy received but Dip was paid $3.00 a week, most of which he sent home to China to pay for his son's education.

Archie Thomas continued to use his wireless, but because his set had limited power, he was only able to communicate with a man named Charles Veeder, a tuberculosis* patient on Cuttyhunk, and with a few ships that passed near the island. In the summer of 1914, with the help of a Boston newspaper, Archie acquired a new wireless.

*A disease that later caused the death of both.

Laundry building, 1996 *Photo: by author*

This set allowed him to transmit messages 50 miles and receive them from over 200 miles away. A radio inspector and a representative from the Marconi Company spent three days on Penikese installing the new equipment and erecting two telegraph poles. These men also taught Archie how to use his new wireless.[5]

When World War I began that year, Archie was able to receive the war news on his wireless from the Marconi News Service. His mother would then type these messages into news bulletins for distribution to the island residents. Archie was also able to contact ships all over the North Atlantic, and thus he and his call letters I.Z.P. became famous. When the Governor of the Commonwealth visited Penikese in August, he was given—to his surprise—Archie's latest world news bulletin.[6]

Frank Pina, one of the first five lepers to arrive on Penikese, died on November 19, 1914. Pina had assisted in the construction of many of the island's buildings and willingly helped, whenever he could, in other work. His health began to fail in 1908 and leprosy gradually weakened his body.

By this time, Penikese had acquired a very dedicated and competent staff. This was no small task as Penikese was, understandably, a difficult place to work. In the first nine years of the colony, 87 full-time employees had been hired, but never more than 10 were on the payroll at one time. Not only was the job of tending to some patients unpleasant, but the solitude on the island and the hostility from the mainlanders and nearby islanders were hard to bear. The total payroll for 1914 amounted to a little over $11,500.[7]

A few days before Christmas that year the residents of Cuttyhunk and the mainland read the news that Penikese Island was being proposed as a national leprosarium. If this proposal was accepted in Congress, all of the nation's lepers would be brought to Penikese.[8] Much to the relief of nearby residents, the idea was abandoned due to the expense of World War I.

At the end of 1914, there were 13 patients on Penikese Island.

16
Succumbing to the Disease
(1915-1917)

During 1915 and 1916, leprosy claimed the lives of seven patients. Leprosy gradually weakened Archie Thomas and he soon contracted tuberculosis. He died on February 17, 1915, at the age of 22. News of his death did not reach the mainland for several days because the weather was bad, and no one knew how to operate Archie's wireless.

Archie was well-liked, and all but two very sick patients attended his funeral service, held at the Hospital. After the service Archie's body was carried to the Island Cemetery in a horse-drawn wagon. Mrs. Thomas and Reverend Bailey led the funeral procession, followed by the Parkers, the staff, and most of the patients, although several could barely walk.[1] Archie's obituary appeared in all the local newspapers, the wireless trade journals, and in Great Britain's *London Times*.[2]

Penikese had not recovered from the death of Archie Thomas when it was further saddened by the death of Isabelle Barros on March 13. Mrs. Barros was one of the original, five lepers and had spent almost ten years on Penikese.

Archie's mother, Emma Thomas, was of course free to leave the island after her son's death, especially since she had not contracted leprosy. At first, she decided to remain and work as a nurse, but the death of her friend Isabelle Barros so closely following her son's death caused Mrs. Thomas to decide to leave. After a short vacation in Maine, the 55-year-old woman settled in Somerville to begin her new life.

The summer of 1915 was a difficult one because of the shortage of fresh water and the large number of flies, mosquitoes, and terns. In June and July, the residents of Penikese were limited to using fresh water only twice a day, for one hour in the morning and one hour in the evening. In the middle of July, 5,000 gallons of fresh water were barreled in New Bedford and shipped to the island. The water problem was again temporarily solved when it finally rained in August.[3]

The swarms of mosquitoes and flies were not only bothersome to the residents, but it was feared that they would spread leprosy to staff persons and animals. The terns, which arrived every year to breed and raise their young, grew to a population of about 5,000 to 7,000 birds. These birds were also a problem because they would attack when they felt their nests were threatened. They would shriek and dive, often clipping the tops of people's heads with their beaks or wing tips. The island's farmer complained that the terns were fouling the hay fields.[4]

Later that year, on October 27, Morris Goldblatt died. He had spent almost eight years on Penikese.

Iwa Umezakia attempted to escape again in 1915, but was stopped before he left the island. The escape attempt was not appreciated by the other patients, as it cost them the privilege of using the small boats. The ban on boat use was lifted the next spring. These boats were used for fishing, and the patients especially enjoyed having their catch cooked for them in the Hospital kitchen.

All patients were now having their meals in the Hospital dining room. No longer did any eat their meals in their cottages. This brought about more interaction between all patients—those in the Hospital and those in their cottages.

At the end of the year, two new patients were admitted to Penikese. There had been no new patients in two years. Nicholas Cacoulaches, 27, arrived on November 18, which was the colony's tenth anniversary. Cacoulaches had immigrated from Greece and had been a dishwasher in Boston. He arrived with obvious signs of leprosy. On December 19, Walton E. Keene, 72, was admitted to Penikese. He was from Bourne and was the oldest patient to be sent to the colony. Keene was a patient for only a little over a month before he died on January 23, 1916. Iwa Umezakia, a colorful and intelligent man, died on January 7, 1916.

Staff and patients of the small island community were obliged to make many adjustments so they could live in a compatible manner. The differences that had to be overcome can best be realized by the description of the funeral of Iwa Umezakia. This funeral was attended by members of the staff, some of whom were not American born, and by about 12 patients of five different nationalities. The funeral service of this Japanese Buddhist, was conducted by a New England Baptist minister.

Dr. James A. Honeij resigned his position as Island Resident Physician on January 31, 1916, and was soon replaced by Dr. William

J. MacDonald, a graduate of Harvard Medical School and a medical researcher. Before he left, Honeij successfully published many articles on leprosy with an associate of his, Dr. Simeon B. Walbach, who was a pathologist at Harvard and a consultant at Penikese.[5]

After he resigned, Dr. Hoenij gave a speech in which he quoted Leontine Lincoln on the subject of leprosy as follows:

> "Surely Massachusetts, the Commonwealth that has ever been foremost in humane and enlightened care of every form of human suffering, will do her utmost to make life as comfortable as possible for these sufferers, and promote every means that has for its object the eradication of this disease that for centuries has been considered incurable and hopeless. Nothing seems impossible to science in our day. May we not confidently hope that even in our generation her faithful students may so far succeed in dealing with this century-dreaded disease that the old cry, 'unclean, unclean,' shall forever be silenced."

The only new patient at Penikese in 1916 was Hassan Hallile, 30, a Mohammedan from Turkey who joined the island colony on April 16. The island staff reported that Hallile spoke no English and that he appeared to be a good-natured person. Later, he became quite depressed and was frequently in tears because he could not provide for his children back in Turkey.

Solomon Goodman died on August 16 at the age of 71. He had lived on Penikese Island for seven years. During his last two years he was very weak and sickly. He was described as a man of gentle disposition and rugged constitution.

For years Lucy Peterson had complained of having throat problems, which was a common ailment among the patients. Suddenly, on November 5 she choked to death. The autopsy revealed that growths on the walls of her throat had enlarged and prevented her from breathing. Lucy Peterson was buried next to her friend, Isabelle Barros. Her grave is marked with a small gravestone.[6]

Reports made that year mentioned that Hyman Klein was no longer using crutches and he enjoyed sleeping out of doors. The mental conditions of patients Flavia Ballentino, Mary Martin, and Wong Quong had deteriorated and each were in various stages of insanity.

In his February, 1917 report,[7] Dr. Parker reflected on the past several years and revealed the amount of concern he had for his patients.

"Many of the early patients were of active disposition. They were energetic. They had their gardens, flower or vegetable, and showed an ambitious desire to excell each other in various activities....Even in their games, sports and walks, the same interest was manifest and the results all contributed to their benefit. Their thoughts being taken off from their own physical conditions they were happier, more contented as a rule; their appetites were better, their sleep sounder and more refreshing. These all aggregating, not only in an impaired physical appearance, but served to increase their individual resisting powers against the savages of the disease.

"While in the end the most of them have succumbed to the disease, their hold on life was actually prolonged, (and you rarely find one but clings to life with the same tenacity as the more fortunate) their unhappy moments have really been shortened and their lives made more endurable by the larger measure of cheerfulness and the greater enjoyment that came to them from their activities.

"Those who were the least active were the first to yield. Of all of our patients, there had rarely been any that has equaled, and none that excelled, Goon Lee Dip and Yee Toy in their love of devotion to the work that has come to their hands. And to-day while the ever increasing manifestations of the disease are ever apparent, that same love of doing something to occupy their minds or their hands is actively present.

"The later arrivals have rarely shown any great desire to and have been very slow to enthuse in, accepting anything that entailed any unusual effort.

"Nine years observations has convincingly shown that the more actively the mind and hands are employed,—the degree of labor being tempered to their individual needs—the happier the patient and more beneficial the result in the treatment."

17
A National Leprosarium
(1917-1920)

The need for a national leprosarium continued to be a concern for those involved in treating people with leprosy. A "Bill to Provide for the Care and Treatment of Lepers"[1] was passed by Congress on February 3, 1917. This bill allowed the federal government to establish a national leprosarium where lepers throughout the nation could be treated. Penikese Island was again considered, but the lack of fresh water caused the investigating committee to look elsewhere.

Through the efforts of Dr. Parker, the Board of Charity, and public officials throughout the country, the federal government purchased, in 1918, the Louisiana Leper Home* in Carville, Louisiana. The federal investigating committee was impressed with the location and facilities of this home, where there were about 100 patients. The Home had been run by The Sisters of Charity for the state of Louisiana since 1896.[2] This purchase delighted the people of Cuttyhunk, though it would not be until 1921 before the national leprosarium opened because of the protests from the Carville area residents.

With the possibility of a national leprosarium opening soon, no new structures were built on Penikese, though buildings were certainly maintained. A new well was dug on the north end of the island and again the fresh water problem solved.

There were three new patients in 1917. Nessem Mecholam, 28, a Turkish Hebrew, arrived on the island on May 20. Mecholam was an active man who spoke several Mediterranean dialects and showed few signs of his disease. However, after two months, he was described by Dr. Parker as a "disturbing element and unfortunate addition to the Colony."** [3]

Hamed Ali, 21, arrived on May 23. He was a Syrian rug salesman from Springfield, who was apprehended by health officials while on a rug-selling trip to Newark, New Jersey and sent back to

---

*Now the United States Public Health Service Gillis W. Long Hansen's Disease Center.

**The author has studied reams of data regarding the leprosarium and these were the only unkind words recorded about any patient on Penikese.

91

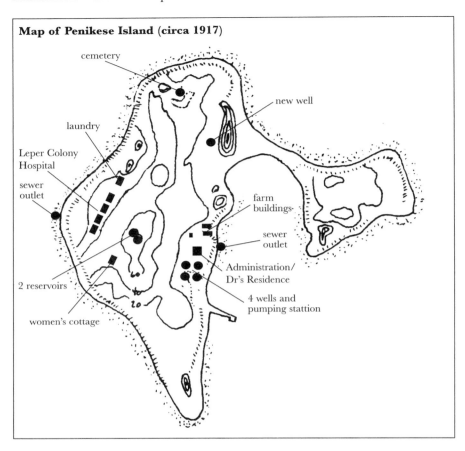

Map of Penikese Island (circa 1917)

cemetery

new well

laundry

Leper Colony
Hospital

sewer
outlet

farm
buildings

sewer
outlet

Administration/
Dr's Residence

2 reservoirs

4 wells and
pumping stattion

women's cottage

Massachusetts. He adjusted easily to the isolated life of Penikese, and people there considered him a pleasant man.

The resident physician, Dr. William J. MacDonald, resigned near the end of May because he was drafted into the Army to serve in World War I. He was not replaced and Dr. Parker, who by this time was receiving $2,500 a year, again took over all responsibilities of the colony and its patients. Marion Parker was able to help her husband with some of the added responsibilities because she now had female inmates from the New Bedford Almshouse to do the housework for them.

During the latter part of World War I and in the years that followed, the hospital suffered from a shortage of help. During the war, medical personnel were interested in assisting the war effort. After the war, it was felt that the national leprosarium would be opening soon, and people were looking for more secure jobs. As a result, record keeping was slack and many things cannot be explained. For example, it is not clear why Julia E. Lowe, 60, an out-of-state resident, was admitted to Penikese on July 24, 1917. She was a resident of Key West, Florida and had an advanced case of leprosy.

There were two deaths on Penikese in 1917—Angeline S. King, Mrs. Parker's mother, and Yee Toy. Mrs. King died on September 25 during one of her frequent trips to the island to visit her daughter. Her body was taken off the island and buried in the Forest Dale Cemetery in Malden.*[4]

In his October report that year, Dr. Parker wrote, "I regret to announce the death of Yee Toy, one of our Chinese patients, on the 23rd Inst. He had been an inmate of the Institution since its inception. He was a good patient; kind and obliging to his fellows: uncomplaining and stoic, he proved himself a faithful follower of Zeno."[5]

There were eight men and three women patients in the hospital colony at the end of 1917.** Aside from leprosy, the general health of the patients was very good. Most of the male patients were receiving injections of Chaulmoogra oil,[6] a new treatment with varying degrees of success. Dip's eyes still bothered him and Cacoulaches had sores in his mouth, though he seemed to be improving. Mrs. Martin had a problem with her legs which required surgery, and Mrs. Lowe gained 13 pounds. All of the patients were taking salt water baths as a treatment; this also helped to conserve fresh water.

Chilin Chiang, 23, arrived on Penikese on June 24, 1918. Chiang was a student from China and was in the early stages of leprosy. He responded well to the treatments given to him at the hospital and was deported to China on November 15.[7] On that same day, John Matthias, 26, was admitted to the island hospital. He was an immigrant from the Cape Verde Islands and his case was not far advanced.

In a report written in early 1919, Dr. Parker stated that there was little change in the conditions of Cacoulaches, Hallile, and Matthias, and he felt that the health of Mrs. Lowe, Wong, and Baptiste was declining. Parker further stated that he saw no signs of improvement in Mrs. Balentino nor Mrs. Martin, but he thought Ali and Klein were doing well. In February, Goon Lee Dip suffered a heart attack, but it was not fatal. Dr. Parker wrote that Dip had a "great reserve power or he would have been dead long ago."[8]

*Gosnold Township records erroneously state that she was buried in the Penikese Island Cemetery.
**They were: Goon Lee Dip, Mary Martin, Flavia Ballentino, Manuiel Baptiste, Wong Quong, Hyman Klein, Nicholas Cacoulaches, Hassan Hallile, Hamed Ali, Nessem Mecholam, and Julia Lowe.

A native of China, Fong Wing, 23, was admitted to Penikese on May 25, 1919. Wing was nicknamed "Jimmy" and had been a waiter in Boston. The only other new patient in 1919 was John Marketakois who arrived on November 8. Marketakois, 24, had immigrated from Greece.

Effective December 1, 1919, supervision of the Penikese Island Hospital was transferred from the Board of Charity to the Department of Public Health, Communicable Diseases Division.[9] This was for administrative purposes and had no effect on the operation of the colony, though the recording keeping was affected. There is very little data available after the Department of Public Health took over the supervision of the hospital. It may have been due to a lack of adequate staffing, but it is certainly the cause of many discrepancies.

Frank Lena, another out-of-state resident, arrived on Penikese Island January 22, 1920. Lena, 24, was from Rome, New York and had been employed at a candy factory.* Nicholas Bruno, an Italian immigrant, who had been employed in Baltimore, Maryland as a "cement worker," was sent to Penikese on February 1.

Nicholas Cacoulaches died on March 12, 1920. He had been a patient at the hospital for five years and had not responded well to medication. His grave is marked with a small granite gravestone.

In April, 1920, two men who had served in the United States Armed Forces were sent to Penikese. These leprous men had been passed from one prison or hospital to another throughout the country for several years. The Massachusetts Legislature, at the federal government's request, unanimously passed a bill that would allow Penikese Island to accept these veterans of World War I.[10] Getulio L. Avelino had served in the United States Navy and was a native of the Philippine Islands. David Ernsberger, 22, was born in India, where his parents were missionaries. At the outbreak of World War I, he quit college and joined the United States Marines. He discovered he had leprosy while he was stationed in Europe. Ernsberger was the last patient to be admitted to Penikese Island.

In July, 1920, Dr. Parker attempted to have two of his patients released. It appears as though he thought that they might have been

---

*Lena's name was an alias. The practice of taking an assumed name was beginning to be the custom with patients of leprosy. Later, at the national leprosarium in Carville, this practice was encouraged to protect patients' families from unwanted notoriety.

cured. Only one of these patients is known—Hyman Klein, who came to Penikese in 1913. The two patients were sent to Boston for further tests, but the tests showed the presence of leprosy and they were returned to Penikese.[11]

None of the patients at Penikese were anxious to leave their island home for the warm, damp climate of Louisiana; they were comfortable on Penikese and had much faith in Dr. Parker's care. They also feared they would not be treated as well as they had been on Penikese. Goon Lee Dip prayed that he would die so he would not have to leave the island, where he had spent about a third of his life. Dip, the last survivor of the original five lepers, died on December 6, 1920. At the time of his death, he was 38 years old, almost blind, and had suffered several heart attacks. For the last five years of his life, he wore special shoes made with thick cotton lining so he could walk on his sore feet. Dip's grave is also marked with a small granite gravestone.

The last patient to die on the island was Julia Lowe, who passed away on December 20, 1920. Mrs. Lowe's general health improved soon after she was admitted to the hospital, but during the three years she lived there the disease took its toll and she became frail and sickly.

18
Penikese Island Hospital Closes
(1921)

In 1921, the national leprosarium became a reality when the United States Public Health Service Hospital (formerly the Louisiana Leper Home) opened in Carville, Louisiana. All the patients on Penikese left the island on March 10, 1921 for the new federal hospital.* The two women and 11 men were transported from Penikese to New Bedford on the tugboat *John T. Sherman*. When they arrived in New Bedford, they were put on a hospital train that was waiting for them at the dock, and then taken to Louisiana.

A local newspaper printed the following account of the arrival of the Penikese patients in New Bedford:

> "The women patients, both victims of the disease in its advance stages, were unable to make the trip over the gangway alone. They were carried by attendants. The men were able to crawl over the gangway aided by deckhands on the tug and were strong enough to carry some of their luggage down the wharf to the waiting car [railway car].
>
> "One of the women [Mary Martin], an inmate for several years, had the first view of her daughter, a resident of New Bedford since the time she departed to the island. It was a pitiful scene, and tried the hearts of many bystanders who were standing around the wharf. Unable to embrace her mother, the daughter was held back by an attendant until she was informed....that she would not be able to talk to her mother until she promised not to embrace or touch her. Consent was readily given and the mother, daughter and other relatives were held aside...
>
> "The second woman, who according to Dr. Frank H. Parker, Resident Physician at the Island, is insane, fell out of a chair which she was being carried...
>
> "Both women were carried down the wharf to the train in a wheelbarrow..."[1]

---

*The patients transferred were: Mary Martin, Flavia Ballentino, Wong Quong, Manuiel Baptiste, Hyman Klein, Hassan Hallile, John Matthias, John Marketokis, Fong Wing, Frank Lena, Getulio Avelino, Nicholas Bruno, and David Ernsberger.

(marginal newspaper column fragments:) beacon / face of / chosen / sacrifice / ler and / has no / for her / I have / the lat- / in the / s until / rkably / malady / s wait- / turned / sweet / ome to / are his / urdens. / far as / to be / rchie" / is pos- / mends.

(image text:) BOY WILL OCCUPY
DR. FRANK H. PARKER AND WIFE

**Dr. Frank H. Parker and wife, Marion, as they appeared in a
newspaper story.** *Source: Harvard's Francis A. Countway Library of Medicine in Boston*

When asked why he did not go to Carville to work with the
patients, Parker replied: "I do not wish to go to Carville because I
prefer to be a big toad in a little pond rather than a little toad in
a big pond."[2]

After the departure of his patients, Dr. Parker returned to
Penikese to attend to the details of closing the hospital. By July, he
had completed his tasks and turned the island over to John Cornell of
Cuttyhunk Island, who was hired by the Department of Health to be
the caretaker for Penikese.[3]

The Penikese Island Hospital had been open for 16 years and had
treated 36 people. Fifteen died, seven were deported, one was
released for treatment elsewhere, and 13 were transferred to
Louisiana. None were cured. Massachusetts taxpayers paid the cost of
the operation, $360,000, which along with specific donations from
private sources made the hospital possible. Harvard University had

assisted by adding visiting pathologists and other medical personnel to the staff.

When Dr. Parker became Superintendent of the island colony, his salary was $2,000 a year. By the time the colony closed, it was $2,500. Mrs. Parker had received a small income as the island's postmaster. When the couple left the island, Dr. Parker was 65 years old and was the state's leading authority on leprosy. Pensions were then given to the state's employees by actions of the legislature and the governor. Governor Cox, however, would not give Dr. Parker a pension because he felt the state had too many pensioners already. The newspapers backed up an effort to get Dr. Parker a pension, but in the end, the Parkers were left to make it on their own.[4]

After their work on Penikese, the Parkers decided to move to Hamilton, Montana to be with their younger son, Dr. Ralph R. Parker. In the winter of 1925-26, there was a whooping cough epidemic in this area and Dr. Parker attended to some of its victims. He contracted this infectious disease and died of complications from it and a weakened heart on January 10, 1926.[6]

Mrs. Parker became active in social and charitable organizations in Montana, as she had been before going to Penikese. Marion Parker died in 1948, and was buried with her husband's ashes in the Riverside Cemetery in Hamilton, Montana.[7]

Upon learning in 1994 of Governor Cox's treatment of Dr. Parker, State Representative Eric Turkington of Falmouth arranged for a plaque honoring Frank and Marion Parker to be permanently displayed at the State House. The plaque reads:

> "In honor of Frank H. Parker, M.D., superintendent Penikese Hospital, Buzzards Bay 1907-1921. And his wife, Marion Parker, for their dedicated service in the care and treatment of those with leprosy. Given on behalf of a grateful Commonwealth by the Department of Health."

When the 13 patients from Penikese arrived at Carville, they were disappointed to find that none of their treatment or personal records accompanied them. They also discovered that conditions there were nothing like those at Penikese. In Carville, there were hundreds of patients and conditions were crowded. Men and women were separated and not even allowed to speak to each other.* The climate was

*This rule was later changed.

hot, humid, and stifling after that of New England.

Mary Martin, Flavia Ballentino, and Wong Quong were unable to give Carville personnel any information because of their mental conditions. Mary Martin died in Carville in 1925, and Flavia Ballentino and Wong Quong both died in 1927.

Manuiel Baptiste escaped from Carville in 1927 and was never heard from again. Hyman Klein was discharged in December, 1921, but returned three years later with ulcers on his feet. Klein died at Carville in 1950 and was the last survivor of the Penikese patients.

Hassan Hallile died in Carville in 1926. John Matthais escaped in September, 1921, not long after he had arrived. John Marketokis escaped two months later in November, 1921. Both were never heard from again. Fong Wing died in Carville in 1934. Frank Lena escaped in January, 1922, was readmitted in 1931, and died in Carville in 1938.

In July 1921, Getulio Avelino escaped. He was the first Penikese patient to do so, but was readmitted in November, 1922, and escaped again in February, 1923. Nicholas Bruno was discharged in April, 1929. David Ernsberger escaped in October, 1922, was readmitted in August, 1923, and married another patient. In September, 1935, he escaped again and was readmitted in August, 1939. He died only a couple weeks later.[5]

19
Penikese Island
Bird Sanctuary (1924-1973)

After Frank Parker left Penikese Island in 1921, the Massachusetts Department of Public Health put the island and its buildings up for sale. The property was assessed at $160,000, but bids of only $20,000, $10,000 and $5,000 were submitted that year. In 1922, another low bid was made.[1] The next year no offers were made. By 1924, the state realized it could not sell the island so they literally gave it "to the birds" by declaring it a bird sanctuary.

In June, 1924, the Massachusetts Legislature passed a bill making Penikese a sanctuary for wild birds.[2] The island then came under the direction of the Department of Conservation, Division of Fisheries and Game. Fred W. Wood, a gamekeeper from the neighboring island of Naushon,[3] was appointed resident caretaker and warden for the new sanctuary. He replaced John Cornell, the caretaker appointed by the Department of Public Health after Dr. Parker left.

The Department of Conservation officially took control of the island in September, 1924. They planned to raise game birds, such as quail and pheasants, and cottontail and snowshoe rabbits. They also wanted to encourage wild ducks, geese, and terns to use the island for protection and breeding.[4] People were no longer allowed to collect tern eggs on the island, then considered a delicacy.

In order to restore the island to a more natural condition, all structures and machinery that Warden Wood did not need had to be destroyed.[5] This decision came after attempts to sell or give away the material were unsuccessful. All the leper colony structures, generators, refrigeration equipment, and farm machinery were in fairly good condition, but the expense of moving the material to the mainland discouraged the few potential buyers. When the material was offered to state institutions and refused, it became clear that no one wanted anything from a former leper colony.

Finding a working crew to come to the island to destroy the buildings was difficult because people feared they would catch leprosy when the buildings were disturbed. In 1925, the state was finally able to contract with a wrecking company from Lowell.[6] This firm got as far as removing the valuable interior wood and roofing from the Administration Building before declaring bankruptcy.*

It was not until November 1926 that Mr. Wood and an official from the Division of Fisheries and Game burned down the wooden structures of the leper colony. This included the cattle shed, the cottages, the Hospital, and the farm buildings. The chicken coop was saved for use as a tool shed. Since the ground was damp, the men did not worry about the fire spreading. When a small fire did start, the men beat it out with a broom. It is interesting to note that Mrs. Wood charged the state 85 cents for her broom that was destroyed during these burnings.[7]

A man named Joseph R. Critchley from Charlemont was hired to dynamite the cement walls of the Administration Building. He destroyed all except the northeast corner which was only several feet from the warden's cottage. They felt that this was too close to be removed by Mr. Critchley's methods and was not removed until 1929.[8] All that remained of the leper colony was the tool shed, the concrete laundry building, the vegetable cellar, and Dr. Parker's laboratory, which had been remodeled into the warden's cottage. In the years that have passed, the cottage and tool shed have rotted away and all that exists today are the concrete walls of the laundry building, the vegetable cellar, and several foundations.

As the buildings on the island were being destroyed, other sections of the land were being prepared for the wildlife. Typha Pond was enlarged and a ditch was dug so that the water from a swamp could run into it, and keep the water level up during dry weather. Different grasses were planted at the edges of the ponds for the birds to feed on. For the quail and pheasants, buckwheat and other grains were planted. While these were growing, special feed was made up and shipped to the island.[9] The snowshoe and cottontail rabbits were protected with new plants of bayberry and wild roses.

Each week Wood kept a record of the activities on the island. On March 25, 1926, he wrote that he saw over 250 ducks and geese fly over the island, many ducks in the ponds, and two cottontail rabbits in the swamp.[10] In just a little over a year, wildlife and game had taken

*About eight years later Harry Turner, the warden at that time, found a small vault on Tubs Point. Thinking it was a pirate's treasure, he forced the lock open only to discover dynamite, which the wrecking crew from Lowell had left behind. He removed the explosives and since then the vault has been washed out of the area by storms.

to the island. Later in the year, he reported that he shot six Great White Owls with wing spans of 24 to 30 inches.[11] These birds were predators of the rabbits and game birds.

In 1927, a particularly dry summer, the ponds and the swamp dried up and the wild grasses died. The wild fowl had to go elsewhere and most did not return the next breeding season. Another disappointment was the failure of the game birds to survive on the island. For some unknown reason, the pheasants' eggs were infertile and these birds gradually died off.[12] The quail were driven away by the ever increasing number of terns, and the snowshoe rabbits ate the shrubs that were planted to protect them. The warden considered these rabbits pests; fortunately, they did not take to the island life and did not multiply.[13] The cottontail rabbits began to multiply but it took many years for them to increase significantly.

In the late 1920's, Mr. Wood resigned as caretaker and warden and was replaced by Harry S. Turner, who moved to the island with his wife and son. At this time, the Division of Fisheries and Game took a close look at its achievements and failures and concluded that the island would be best utilized if they concentrated on wild water birds and cottontail rabbits. The warden began attracting more ducks and geese with the use of food and live decoy birds. Gradually, the number of wild water birds increased.

Up to this time, the Division of Fisheries and Game had been buying cottontail rabbits from various other states because there was a shortage of them in Massachusetts. Several diseased rabbits had been imported to the state and this disease spread and killed off many local rabbits. To prevent this from recurring, the Division organized the cottontail rabbit propagation station on Penikese Island.[14] In addition to his work with the wild water birds, Turner took considerable time establishing cottontails on the island. His success was slow but after trying many methods, he was finally able to raise enough healthy rabbits to ship some to areas in the state where rabbits had died out.

In order to protect the young birds and rabbits, Warden Turner needed to shoot their predators, the owls and hawks. However, the hawk is also the natural predator of the snake. Penikese Island has two varieties of snakes, the Dekay snake and the garter snake.[15] It is not known for certain how these snakes first came to the island, but it is suspected that they have been there since the glacier receded from the area and were trapped on the island when the ocean levels rose.

Others suspect that the snakes were brought to the island for experimental purposes by the Anderson School and released when the school closed. During the week of April 15-23, 1932, Mr. Turner reported he killed 550 garter snakes.[16] Today there is an above average number of snakes on Penikese, but an occasional hawk and breeding sea gulls keep their numbers somewhat in check.

Mr. and Mrs. Turner had frequent visitors to the island to study the various forms of flora and wildlife there. Studies of the flora and a check on the number of different plants had been going on since the Anderson School opened in 1873. At that time, there were 108 different species; in 1923, 166 species; in 1947, 158 species; and in 1973, 163 species. Penikese Island is probably the most consistently studied area on the east coast in this field. [17]

For many years specially-licensed people had put identifying bands on young sea birds found on Penikese. In July, 1932, these "bird-banders" spent three days on the island and were only able to band 490 young terns because many of the tern eggs had not yet hatched. They returned ten days later and were astonished to find that of the approximately 7,000 adult terns they had seen on their previous trip, only about 500 were left. They were also amazed to discover that the baby terns they had banded were missing; only one dead bird was found. There were very few eggs and these were scattered out of their nests. Warden Turner was also astonished. He reported that during the ten days that the "bird-banders" were away, there was no unusual activity on the island and he noticed no sudden decrease in the number of adult birds. This mystery has never been solved, however the adult terns returned the following year to nest and raise their young.*[18]

In the summer of 1933, a man named Dr. Townsend discovered that the Leach's Petrel (or Storm Petrel) were nesting on the island. Previous to this, there was no known nesting area of this nocturnal sea bird south of Maine. The Petrels built their nests underground behind a stone retaining wall where they were safe from the gulls.[19] When Dr. Townsend's discovery of these birds was reported, another man tried to authenticate it and began to remove a portion of the wall. He was stopped by Warden Turner before he disturbed any nests. The island's present tenants (The Penikese Island School), who

*In 1933, a small colony of Herring Gulls were noticed on the island. By 1973, thousands of Herring Gulls were nesting and only a small colony of terns. In 1978, the "bird-banders" found that the gulls had taken over all the nesting areas and no terns were present.

106

are zealous in protecting the nesting area, believe that these birds are increasing. One of the island occupants complained that he was once hit by a flying Petrel while he was on an evening walk.[20]

In 1938, a hurricane destroyed most of the island's structures and boats. The pier was completely demolished, leaving only the stone portion. The boathouses were awash and an old truck floated out of one. The island's boats were washed ashore and the Turner's cottage roof was ruined when the chimney fell in. Rain destroyed the ceilings as well as the furnace in the cellar. The rabbit traps and hutches were either wrecked or blown away and some of the rabbits were killed. On Tubs Point, then called Point Agassiz, there was one large fresh water pond. The seas washed over the area, reduced the size of the point and left only a small pond. The Division of Fisheries and Game helped Warden Turner restore his cottage and rebuilt some of the island's buildings. The rabbit structures were replaced and Warden Turner soon had his station in good condition.

Another tragedy occurred in July, 1941. On July 6, Mr. and Mrs. Turner and several visiting relatives went to the mainland for the day. Louise Turner, the Turner's granddaughter, and another child stayed behind with an adult. While the children were playing a hunting game in the house, Louise Turner was fatally shot by the other child with the warden's gun. Later at a hearing in New Bedford, the incident was ruled an accident and no charges were filed.[21]

It was soon after this incident that the Department of Fisheries and Game closed the rabbit propagation station. They felt that the cottontail rabbits had multiplied sufficiently throughout the state and there was no longer any need to maintain the rabbit propagation work. The birds had also increased to significant numbers throughout the area and those which nested on the island would be protected by laws that prohibit hunting in a sanctuary. At the end of 1941, the Turners left the island and Mr. Turner began a new position on the mainland with the Division of Fisheries and Game. For the first time in 300 years, Penikese was uninhabited.

The island remained unoccupied for 32 years. Employees of the Division of Fisheries and Game occasionally went there to check on the bird population and a few people came to study the flora and to band birds, but most of the time the island was unattended. Often it was used for illegal activities, such as hunting and camping.

Even though Turner no longer lived there, he occasionally visited the island to check on the property. On August 10, 1942, he found the island posted with signs that read:

> "Warning! United States Army, Eastern Military Area. Under the authority of the executive order 9066 of the President of the U.S. and pursuant to the public proclamation issued by the headquarters of the Eastern Defense Command and First Army, Governor's Island N. Y. and the within area has been designated a Restricted Zone. Copies of this proclamation can be obtained at any P. O. within the Eastern Military Area.
>
> H.A. Drum, Lt. General, U.S. Army."

During World War II, when an area was posted as a restricted zone, civilians were not allowed within the area. Penikese was restricted because Gull Island—a very small island about a half a mile away—was used as a target during practice bombing, and officials feared Penikese could be hit accidentally.

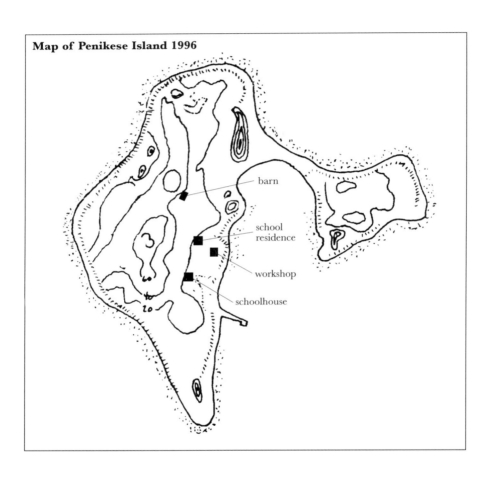

Map of Penikese Island 1996

barn

school
residence

workshop

schoolhouse

110

20
Penikese Island School
(1973-present)

In 1973, the Department of Conservation, Division of Fisheries and Wildlife, was approached by four men from the Woods Hole area about opening a private rehabilitation school on Penikese for teenage delinquent boys. George Cadwalader, Herman Bosch, David Masch, and Carl Jackson persuaded the Wildlife officials to agree to their proposal. They also requested that the Massachusetts Audubon Society investigate whether or not their proposed school, and activities connected with it, would interfere with the wildlife. The Audubon Society authorities later determined that the proposed school would not interfere with wildlife programs because the acreage involved was not heavily nested by breeding gulls. They also felt that the presence of the school would protect the island from illegal hunters and campers. This, in turn, would enhance the sanctuary's value.

The Penikese Island School was officially established in July, 1973. The school then signed a contract to lease 11 acres of Penikese Island from the Division of Fisheries and Wildlife.[1] The first student arrived in August, 1973, and was quickly followed by six others. These students and the staff were able to construct the framework for the school's main building on the leper colony's cattle barn foundation and enclose the building before the school closed for the winter.

In the 1974 summer session, the students and staff finished the main building and built a barn and bunkhouse. The new barn was constructed on a foundation that once held a barn built by John Anderson in 1867. In 1976 and 1977, a woodworking shop was built on the foundation of the warden's cottage,[2] which had been Dr. Parker's laboratory prior to that. Since then, a schoolhouse and several more farm buildings have been added.

Now open year-round, the Penikese Island School is one of the oldest residential programs for delinquents in Massachusetts. Students tend the farm and learn woodworking, boat building, and other types of construction; they study nature firsthand and continue their schooling in an informal manner.

George Cadwalader describes 14 years of the school's history, from 1973 to 1986, in his book *Castaways* (Chelsea Green Publishing Company, Chelsea, Vermont, 1988). His idea for the school began when he worked as an administrator at the Oceanographic Institute in Woods Hole. He was discontent with his desk job and knew he did not have the math and science background to participate in the research that was going on around him. However, he did enjoy the Oceanographic research cruises and considered contacting the Outward Bound program to see about job possibilities there. When he mentioned this to his boss, Fred Mangelsdorf, Mangelsdorf suggested that he open his own school and mentioned that Massachusetts was in the process of replacing its juvenile delinquent reform schools with private programs. The conversation took place on a plane from New York to Boston. As Cadwalader pondered this idea, he looked out the window at the Elizabeth Islands and wondered if one of these islands might be a good place for his school. When he returned to Woods Hole, he began working towards his dream.[3]

Cadwalader's story of his many years trying to rehabilitate juvenile delinquents is similar in some ways to Dr. Parker's experiences. Dr. Parker spent 15 years trying to cure his patients of leprosy and never succeeded. In the end, Parker found that he had to be content knowing that he had at least improved the health of many patients and added months or years to their lives. Cadwalader, who always wanted to be a doctor, has found that delinquency is also hard to "cure." Of the first 106 boys who attended the Penikese Island School (from 1973 to 1980), only 16 of them had "turned themselves around." The rest had gone on to lead destructive lives, committing 309 violent crimes and 3,082 nonviolent crimes. Cadwalader knows these results are typical of other rehabilitation programs. For those students who continue to commit crimes and may sit behind bars now, he believes that the school has added a few good moments to their lives and perhaps some fond memories to reflect upon.[4]

The Penikese Island School has weathered many financial hardships over the years. The politics in the Massachusetts juvenile delinquent system also affects the operations of the school. In the early 1980s, after the disappointing study on the 106 boys was completed, the school suffered a particularly difficult period. Cadwalader was ready to give up, and began developing a plan for razing the buildings, in order to restore the island to its original state.[5] During his planning, he discovered that many people did not want the school closed, and money was found to keep the school running. As of August, 1997, the Penikese Island School was still in operation on a year-round basis.

Penikese Island School, 1996 *Photo: by author*

Appendix

Reported Cases of
Leprosy in Massachusetts
(1825-1920)*

In 1882, state health officials began applying numbers to cases of leprosy. Prior to that date there were only four reported cases and very little is known about them. The author has assigned these early cases a case letter for easy identification.

Case A: Reported in 1825.

Case B: Reported in 1870.

Case C: Reported in the mid-1870s (possibly 1875).

Case D: Reported in 1880. Charles Wilson, 30. Cuban. Reported to have leprosy while he was a patient at the Massachusetts General Hospital, where he had a foot amputated. He left the state in 1884.[1,2]

Case #1. **Charles Derby**. Single. Born in Salem, Massachusetts. Contracted leprosy while he was a botanist and gardener for the Queen of the Sandwich Islands (Hawaiian Islands). Derby knew he had leprosy and returned to Salem in 1882 to be cared for by his family. State health officials were notified of this case in December and they reported that his disease was "very evident." Derby's body was covered with ulcers, his voice was altered by the disease, and he was blind in one eye. He was then sent to the Salem Almshouse (poorhouse) where he lived in the attic until a special cottage was built for him. He died in this cottage in March, 1883. [1,2,15]

Case #2. Name unknown. Female. Swedish. In 1889,** this fairly advanced case was discovered at the quarantine station in Boston. She was taken from the bark *Samaria* and deported without landing in this country.[15]

Case #3. Name unknown. Male. This American sailor had lived in East Boston for only a few months before he was diagnosed with leprosy in September, 1895. Before he moved to Boston, he had worked aboard a ship that carried lepers to the Molokai Leper Colony in the Hawaiian Islands. This man was isolated at Gallops Island where he died in 1897.[15]

Case #4. Name and sex unknown. This person was discovered in Boston in 1900 and died at Gallops Island.[15]

Case #5. Name and age unknown. Male. It is not clear from records whether this man was named Baker or whether this was his occupation. This black native of the British West Indies lived   the West End of Boston. He went to the Massachusetts Eye and Ear Infirmary because of a sore eye, and it was discovered there that he had leprosy. He was sent to Gallops Island and escaped on May 8, 1903. He was never found.[1,15]

---

*References for this section can be found on page 127.

**The author feels this date should read 1884 because it is out of sequence. However, records read 1889.

Penikese Island Leper Colony opens November 18, 1905.

The following information provides more detailed biographical descriptions on the patients of Penikese Island. The number, after the name of each patient, refers to the age at which he or she was diagnosed. Variations on the spelling of a name appear in parentheses.

Case #6. **Frank Pina,** 38. Native of the Cape Verde Islands. He and his wife immigrated to New Bedford on the Schooner *Sea Fox*. They lived in South Dennis for three years and then moved to Harwich, where they spent nine years raising eight children. Pina was diagnosed with leprosy on April 21, 1904, by Dr. Louis Edmonds of Harwich. Health officials required Mrs. Pina and her children to leave, and live in another part of town. Pina was cared for in his home by Dr. Edmonds and a nurse; a neighbor was hired to bring food and supplies to the house. Medical expenses, supplies and rent, which averaged $8.00 a day, were paid for by the town.

The expense of Pina's care, coupled with the fear of the disease, caused town officials to consider moving Pina to Gallops Island. However, towns along the route to Gallops Island would not allow persons with contagious diseases to be transported through their villages. This dilemma caused health officials to sponsor a bill in the legislature that would permit persons with contagious diseases to be transported by private methods from any point in the Commonwealth to an isolation center. While this bill was being drawn up, the Penikese colony opened and Pina was secretly transported to Fairhaven and then Penikese. Pina arrived with four other leprous people on November 18, 1905, the first day Penikese Island Leper Colony opened. In Harwich, the local newspaper, the *Harwich Independent*, ran an editorial that was headlined "Harwich Rid of Its Leper."

After Pina was settled on the island, the state reimbursed the Town of Harwich for the expense of caring for the man. The state also agreed to pay Pina's landlord the assessed value of the cottage where Pina had lived and have it destroyed.

Under treatment at Penikese Island, Pina showed remarkable improvement and had excellent health other than leprosy. He willingly helped in the island's work and assisted in building some of the island's structures. Pina's health began to fail in 1908 and he died November 19, 1914. He was buried in the Island Cemetery. [1, 3, 04, 05, 06, 07, 08, 15, 25]

Case #7. **Goon Lee Dip** (Goon S. Dub, Goon S. Dip), 23. Chinese. Known on the island as "Willie Goon," "The Chinaman," or "Lee." Dip claimed he was born in the United States, married in China, left his wife and son in China, and returned to this country in 1902. He lived two years in Roxbury, where he worked in a laundry. On June 6, 1904, he was diagnosed with leprosy and sent to Gallops Island. Dip was one of the first five lepers sent to Penikese Island on November 18, 1905. He was described as "able-bodied, content and willing to work," popular with the other patients and staff, and "cheerful even under the most trying conditions." In 1907, he cut off his queue as a token of good feelings toward the United States. He also grew a mustache much like that of Dr. Parker's. In 1915, he was put in charge of the new laundry. In this position, he earned $3.00 a week, which he sent to China for the education of his son. By 1917, Dip's eyes began to bother him and he spent many days in darkened rooms. He died on December 6, 1920, four

118

months before the colony closed. His grave in the Island Cemetery is marked with a granite gravestone.[04, 05, 06, 07, 15, 25]

Case # 8. **John Roderick** (Roderiques, Rodergross), 34. Single. Sailor. Native of the Cape Verde Islands. He was diagnosed as leprous on August 14, 1904. He spent one week on Gallops Island, and then escaped. Five months later he was diagnosed again at the Chelsea Marine Hospital, and sent back to Gallops Island. He was one of the first five lepers to arrive on Penikese Island, on November 18, 1905. He was described as "very sick and slowly dying." Eight members of his family had leprosy. Roderick died on June 21, 1907, the first leper to die on Penikese and to be buried in the Island Cemetery.[1, 04, 05, 06, 07, 15, P]

Case #9. **Yee Toy,** 25. Single. Chinese. Immigrated to the United States in 1900. He spent four years in Newburyport, working in a laundry. On January 18, 1905, he was diagnosed as leprous and sent to Gallops Island. He was one of the first five lepers sent to Penikese on November 18, 1905. In time, he became the stereotypic leper, with disfigured limbs and ulcers all over his face. He also suffered from "fits" and gonorrhea. In 1907, Toy, like his friend Dip, cut off his queue. He was described as "a spirited, courageous person who liked to keep busy." Toy died on October 23, 1917 and is buried in the Island Cemetery.[05, 06, 07, 13N,15, 17, 17F, 25]

Case #10. **Isabelle Barros,** 27. Native of the Cape Verde Islands. She was diagnosed on April 24, 1905, and remained isolated in her Wareham home until the Penikese Colony opened on November 18, 1905. Her husband, Napoleon Barros, acted as nurse while their two small children were placed in a foster home. Mrs. Barros was one of the first five lepers (and the only female) to arrive on Penikese on Opening Day. She was described as "weak, anemic, and debilitated." Mrs. Barros suspected her father of having leprosy. After five months, she gave birth to a healthy baby boy on March 8, 1906. She kept the baby for only 20 days and then had to turn him over to the Board of Charity. The boy, Leontine Lincoln Barros, joined his brother and sister in a foster home. Mrs. Barros' health improved greatly in the first year on the island. In September of 1906, Dr. Edmonds erroneously stated that he had cured Barros and would send her home. This was soon proven false and signs of leprosy returned. Mrs. Barros remained on the island until she died on March 13, 1915. She is buried in the Island Cemetery.[1, 05, 06, 07, 08, 15, 24, 25, P]

Case #11. **Charles W. Beals,** 54. Born in New Orleans, Louisiana. He was from Hyde Park and spent 18 years in Massachusetts with his wife and two children. (He became a widower while he was on Penikese.) Beals was suspected of being leprous on October 29, 1906, and was held for seven months on Gallops Island for tests. These tests proved positive and he was sent to Penikese on May 31, 1907. Beals had never left the country and thought he might have contracted the disease from handling foreign money as an accountant for an express company. (Health officials didn't feel this was viable.) He died on November 7, 1912 and his body was taken to Boston for burial. He was the only leper taken off the island for internment.[06, 07, 15, 24]

Case #12. **Joseph Needham,** 23. Unmarried. Clerk. Immigrated to New York in 1904 from Trinidad, West Indies. He moved to Montreal, Canada and later to Somerville, where he lived a short time before being sent to Penikese on May 31, 1907. His case was in its advance stages. Later that year, he was described as steadily improving and the sores on his face were healing. In 1908, these ulcers returned to his face, his eyes became infected, and he had to stay in a dimly lit room for many weeks. In 1912, he wrote the following letter while recovering from pneumonia:

> Penikese, Mass.
> 10th, Oct. 1912
> Dr. Frank H. Parker
> Supt. Penikese Island, Mass.
>
> My Dear Dr.
> I wish to express my very best thanks and appreciation to you and your wife for all the kindness and good treatment I have received from you both since you have been here. I hope and trust that you and yours will be together with us for many years to come. With all good wishes and success to you.
>
> Yours very sincerely,
> Joseph Needham

Needham died on August 8, 1913. As he requested, a Catholic priest attended his burial in the Island Cemetery. Needham may have also have been called Frank Fanuvela.[07, 08, 15, 25, P]

Case #13. **Lucy Peterson,** 27. Single. Miss Peterson was of Latvian heritage, born in Russia where her parents and three sisters lived. When she immigrated to this country in 1900, she had a brother who lived in Concord and an uncle in Cambridge. Miss Peterson worked as a domestic in Concord for over four years and then moved to Brookline where she also worked. On July 22, 1907, she was declared a leper by health officials and sent to Penikese two days later. On arrival at the colony, she was described as "pretty and well formed." Miss Peterson kept the other patients' cottages clean and often acted as nurse, and sometimes interpreter, for which she received $2.00 weekly. She was very friendly and encouraged others as much as she could. By 1913, she was described as comely but with a "lion's face." (The cartilage in her nose had become affected by leprosy and her nose had flattened.) Lucy Peterson died suddenly on November 5, 1916. An autopsy showed that growths in her throat had enlarged, therefore cutting off her ability to breathe. Lucy Peterson was buried in the Island Cemetery, beside her friend Isabelle Barros, and her grave is marked with a small granite gravestone. Reverend Bailey held burial services on November 8.[07, 15, 25, P]

Case #14. **Morris Goldblatt,** 41. Immigrated from Russia in 1903. Goldblatt lived in Lynn with his wife and five children and worked in a leather factory. Then he moved to East Boston, where he was diagnosed as leprous. He arrived on Penikese on August 29, 1907. His case was in its advanced stages; he had large ulcers on one arm and partial loss of sensation in both arms and on his nose. There is very little information about Goldblatt's life on the island but on May 2, 1915, a reporter from *The Boston Globe* visited the island and wrote that Goldblatt's hands were bandaged and that he asked Dr. Parker for gloves. The article goes on to say: "The Doctor told us about Morris. He sits crying by the hour because he doesn't hear from his family. Some of them visited the island last summer and nearly went into hysteria upon leaving him. Since then, they haven't written a word and Morris rocks back and forth in his corner of the hospital waiting for a letter." Morris Goldblatt died on Penikese October 27, 1915 and is buried in the Island Cemetery. [07, 15, 25, P]

Case #15. **Bertha Osis,** 19. Single. Latvian. Born in Courland, Russia. Miss Osis came to this country in 1905 and worked in Brookline. She was diagnosed with leprosy on December 2, 1907, and was on Penikese 24 hours later. Because she had not lived in the United States long enough to acquire citizenship and had the disease before she came to the United States, she had to be deported. Health officials, however, wanted to be certain of their diagnosis so they retained her on Penikese for six months. (The only visible sign of the disease was a small spot on her cheek, and she was described as "beautiful.") Miss Osis did not want to go to Russia and hoped to stay at Penikese under the care of Dr. Parker. When her condition was confirmed, the law required her to leave. On May 10, 1908, she was put on the New York-bound freighter *Ramona* in New Bedford. The crew of this ship required Miss Osis to stay downwind of them; otherwise, they would curse at her and yell "Leper." In New York Harbor, small boats and tugs circled the *Ramona* with their crews and passengers, eager to see the young woman. Miss Osis was transferred to the steamer *Hellig Olav*, the same ship that brought her to the United States, and was taken back to Russia. [07, 08, 15, P]

Case #16. **Soloman Goodman,** 64. Hebrew. Immigrated from Russia with his wife and two children in 1889. Goodman was from the North End in Boston and taught Hebrew to children. For three years he had trouble walking and was treated for fallen arches. When his problem was found to be caused by leprosy, he was sent to Penikese on March 27, 1909. In 1913, his condition had improved and he was described as having a rugged constitution and as being rarely depressed. By mid-1915, however, he was described as very sick and dying. Solomon Goodman died on August 16, 1916, at the age of 71 and is buried in the Island Cemetery. [09, 15, 25, P]

Sometime between 1904 and 1909 a leprous female from the West Indies escaped from authorities in Fall River, Massachusetts. It is suspected that she returned to her native country. She was not retained long enough to be assigned a case number. [09]

Case #17. **Archibald James B. Thomas,** 16. Immigrated from Barbados, West Indies in February, 1902 with his mother when he was nine years old. His father was not allowed to enter the states because of a skin disease (most likely leprosy) and was returned to Barbados, where he died a few years later. "Archie" had no brothers or sisters. He and his mother lived in Upton where Mrs. Thomas was a supervisor in a hat factory and Archie attended the local school. Archie was considered a good student; his interests were in physics, electricity and the wireless telegraph. When Archie developed a skin rash, Mrs. Thomas took him to a Boston hospital where he was found to have leprosy. He was isolated for five days and then sent to Penikese Island on March 27, 1909. Mrs. Thomas joined her son on the island after she was given permission to do so by the Board of Charity. She lived with him in his cottage and was given a position as Nurse's Assistant at a salary of $200 a year. She had complete freedom of the island and could visit the mainland whenever she pleased. Archie had his own wireless set on the island and his call letters, I.Z.P., became famous. Archie Thomas died on February 17, 1915, at the age of 22 from tuberculosis. His obituary appeared in all the local newspapers, wireless trade journals, and the *London Times*.[2, 09, 12A, 15, 25, 28, P]

Case #18. **Demetrias Phresa** (Phresca), 25. Single. Immigrated from Greece in 1907. He worked as a cook in Haverhill, where his case was first diagnosed as impetigo contagiosa. While he was a patient at the state infirmary in Tewksbury, doctors diagnosed his illness as leprosy. He arrived on Penikese the same day that he was diagnosed, April 24, 1909. Dr. Parker stated that he caused discipline problems on the island, was short-tempered, and once wounded another patient with a knife. Phresa was deported on October 15, 1909 because he had not acquired citizenship. However, he refused to leave and had to be restrained with ropes when he was taken to New York aboard the *Andrew G. Pierce*. He understood little English and thought he was being returned to Greece to be tried for murder. Once in New York, they placed him on the steamer *Argentina* and he was deported to Greece.[09, 15, P]

Case #19. **Mary Martin** (Martinez), 44. Widow. Born in Brava, Cape Verde Islands. Immigrated to New Bedford on May 5, 1902, where she lived with her married daughter and was employed as a cook. On December 14, 1909 she was diagnosed with leprosy and was quarantined in her home with a police guard until she went to Penikese several days later. Her home was fumigated with special gases before her daughter was allowed to return. Martin steadfastly denied she had leprosy, which was not uncommon for people with this disease. Over time, she gradually lost her mind. She spent 12 years on the island before she was transferred to the Carville hospital on March 10, 1921. She died there in 1925.[09, 15, 26, P]

Case #20. **John Anthony**, 23. Single. Laborer. Anthony was a Syrian who immigrated to the United States in 1906. He lived in a North Adams tenement house when he was diagnosed as a leper on May 19, 1910. He was isolated in his apartment, put under police guard, but escaped and was never heard from again.[15, P]

Case #21. **Iwa Umezakia**, 26. Single. Japanese. Carpenter and cabinet maker. He had immigrated to the United States through Seattle, where he helped build a mansion. Later he moved to Boston, where he was employed by Mrs. Jack Gardner to assist in building her mansion.* While living in Boston, he was diagnosed as leprous and sent to Penikese on January 26, 1911. He was described as being "short, of light build, of considerable intelligence and antisocial towards the other patients." Umezakia was very unhappy on Penikese and brooded over the Japanese government's refusal to allow him to return to Japan so he could die among his family. He made an unsuccessful escape from the island, once rowing 14 miles to Padanaram and then taking the train to Boston. He was returned to Penikese and died a few years later on January 7, 1916. He is buried in the Island

*Now the Isabella Stewart Gardner Museum in Boston.

Cemetery in an unmarked grave. Reverend Bailey officiated at his funeral.[15, 25, P]

In May, 1911, a 15-year-old boy named Harry Sheridan from Pawtucket, Rhode Island was found to have leprosy while he was a patient at the Massachusetts General Hospital. The boy was taken back to Rhode Island by his parents who isolated him and refused to turn him over to authorities. He was never in the custody of the Massachusetts Board of Health, nor was he ever on Penikese.[P]

Case #22. **Flavia Ballentino,** 47. Immigrated to the United States from Italy in 1907. She and her husband lived in Boston's North End for four years before she developed a rash, which was first diagnosed as smallpox. Mrs. Ballentino was isolated at Massachusetts General Hospital, where tests showed her disease to be leprosy. She arrived on Penikese on May 15, 1911, and found it very difficult to adjust to her new surroundings. During the 10 years she spent on Penikese, her mind slowly deteriorated until she was considered completely insane. Mrs. Ballentino was transferred to the Carville hospital in 1921, where she died in 1927.[15, 26, P]

Case #23. **Elais Applebaum,** 55. Married. Hebrew. Eight children. Immigrated from Russia. He lived in Boston's South End and worked as a painter for 16 years before moving to Roxbury, where he spent four years. He arrived on Penikese on May 11, 1912. Applebaum's family was considerably upset and was able to have him discharged from the colony on March 21, 1913, "for treatment elsewhere."[15, P]

Case #24. **Henry Chin Yen,** 30. Married. Chinese. He lived in China with his wife and son before he immigrated to the United States in 1902. Other than seven months in Providence, Rhode Island, and two days in Boston, it is not know where else Yen lived. He arrived on Penikese on June 15, 1912 and responded so well to treatment that the visible signs of the disease disappeared. He was released from Penikese on January 3, 1914 and allowed to return to China.

Case #25. **Marion J. Braga,** 34. Single. Born in the Azores and immigrated to New Bedford in 1910. He lived in the New Bedford Almshouse where he acted as a fireman. After being diagnosed as leprous, Braga was sent to Penikese on June 28, 1912. Because he was not a citizen of the U.S., he was deported on August 13, 1912.[15, P]

Case #26. **Manuiel C. Baptiste** (Manueil Corriea), 24. Single. Immigrated from the Cape Verde Islands in 1908 and settled in Norton. Baptiste was employed as a cranberry bog worker and a laborer in various towns throughout southeastern Massachusetts. While waiting for a ship to leave New Bedford for the Cape Verde Islands, Baptiste was apprehended by health officials and found to be leprous. He was planning to return to his homeland to be married. He was sent to Penikese on November 10, 1912. Baptiste lived on the island until it closed in 1921, and was then transferred to the Carville hospital. He escaped from there in 1927 and was never heard from again.[15, 17F, 26, P]

Case #27. **Wong Quong,** 38. Single. Immigrated to San Francisco in 1908. He was a waiter and cook in Boston's Chinatown for over a year before being sent to Penikese Island on March 13, 1913. His condition was described as well-advanced. Quong was transferred to Carville where it was reported they could not get a case history from him because of his mental condition. He died at the Carville hospital in 1927.[15, 26]

Case #28. **Hyman Klein,** 26. Single. Hebrew. Born in the Baltic Province of Russia. Klein immigrated to Boston in 1906, where he had an uncle and two brothers. He lived in Boston for about six years and worked as a brush maker. Klein had just moved to a boarding house in Malden when he was diagnosed a leper and sent to Penikese on November 12, 1913. His leprosy was described as the tubercular form and he had a number of ulcers on his throat and nose. In 1920, Dr. Parker thought Klein had been cured and sent him to Boston for tests. The tests proved the continued presence of leprosy so Klein was returned to Penikese. When Penikese closed, he was transferred to Carville, where he wrote articles under the name Hyman Small. He was discharged from Carville in December, 1921, but returned three years later with ulcers on his feet and complaining that he could not earn a living. Klein died at the Carville Hospital in 1950, the last survivor of the Penikese Island patients.*[15, 17J, 26, 29, P]

Case #29. **Nicholas Cacoulaches,** 27. Single. Immigrated from Greece in 1911. Employed as a dishwasher in a Boston restaurant. After his diagnosis, he was held for 10 days in Boston and then sent to Penikese on November 18, 1915, the colony's tenth anniversary. He had "very obvious" signs of leprosy. Calcoulaches did not respond well to treatment and died on March 12, 1920. He was buried in the Island Cemetery, where his grave is marked with a granite gravestone.[15, 25]

Case #30. **Walton E. Keene,** 72 (the oldest patient sent to Penikese). Married. One child. Born in 1843. It was impossible to tell where Keene might have contracted leprosy because he had led a very active life. From 1865 to 1872, he hunted for gold in the Rocky Mountains; from 1872 to 1876, he was in the shoe business in Brockton; in 1878 and 1879, he explored South America; for four years, he was a sailor on the Pacific Coast; from 1882 to 1899, he was a storekeeper in Bourne; and from 1909 to 1911, he was employed by the town's Gypsy Moth Commission. Keene was diagnosed as a leper at Massachusetts General Hospital and sent to Penikese on December 19, 1915, where he was described as "aged and infirm." It is not clear how he was transported from Boston to Penikese because of his condition. He may have boarded a ship in Boston. If so, Keene would have passed through the Cape Cod Canal and through his hometown of Bourne. Keene died a month after arriving at Penikese, on January 23, 1916, and was buried in the Island Cemetery.[15, 16, 25, P]

Case #31. **Hassan Hallile,** 30. Widower. Mohammedan. Three children. Immigrated from Turkey in 1913. Nothing is known about his three years in the states before coming to Penikese on April 16, 1916. The island staff reported that Hallile spoke no English and was "respectful and obedient." He was depressed most of the time and was frequently in tears because he could not provide for his children, whom he had left in Turkey. He was transferred to Carville, where he died in 1926.[16, 16A, 26, P]

Case #32. **Porfias Diaz**, 20. Single. Student. Born in Cuba, came to the United States in 1915, entered a prep school and in August, 1916 after some discomfort went to Massachusetts General Hospital in Boston where he was diagnosed

*Klein was the man who wrote the story about the grounded sailor who came to his cottage one night looking for help.

124

with leprosy. His parents were notified and he was deported to Cuba. This man was never at Penikese.[16, P]

Case #33. **Nessem Mecholam,** 28. Single. Hebrew. Immigrated from Turkey in 1913 before going to Central America for two years. He then returned to the states to live with a cousin in Salem. He lived in Salem less than a year when he was diagnosed as leprous and sent to Penikese on May 20, 1917. Mecholam was an active man who spoke several Mediterranean dialects and showed few signs of his disease. He was described as a "disturbing element and unfortunate addition to the Colony." There are no mentions of this man after 1918; it is assumed that he was deported.[17, 17J, 17M, P]

Case #34. **Hamed Ali** (Hamed Alla), 21. Single. Syrian. Born in Jerusalem. Ali immigrated to the United States in May, 1914. He drifted around the country and then settled in Springfield, where he became a rug salesman. He was apprehended by health officials while he was selling rugs in Newark, New Jersey. New Jersey authorities returned Ali to Springfield, and he arrived on Penikese Island on May 23, 1917. Ali adjusted easily to the isolated life and he was considered a pleasant man. According to records, he was on Penikese until at least January 1, 1921. It is assumed that he was either deported or released because there are no records to indicate his death or transfer.[17, 17J, P]

Case #35. **Julia E. Lowe,** 60. Widow. Resident of Key West, Florida. Lowe had lived all her life in Florida before she arrived on Penikese on July 24, 1917. There are no records to explain why this out-of-state resident was admitted. She had an advance case of leprosy and, like the other patients, she improved for several years and then slowly declined. Julia Lowe died on December 20, 1920, and was buried in the Island Cemetery.[17, 25]

Case #36. Name unknown. This man was being tested at a hospital when he evidently became aware of his condition and escaped from authorities. He was never heard from again.[18]

Case #37. **Chilin Chiang,** 23. Student. Native of China. Chiang arrived on Penikese on June 24, 1918 and was found to be in the early stages of leprosy. He responded well to treatment and was deported to China on November 15, 1918.[18, 19]

Case #38. **John Matthias** (Mathias), 26. Single. Immigrated from the Cape Verde Islands in 1912. He arrived at Penikese Island on November 15, 1918. His case was described as "not far advanced." He was sent to Carville in 1921, escaped from there September, 1921, and was never heard from again.[18, 26]

Case #39. **Fong Wing,** 23. Married. Native of China. Wing left his wife in China and immigrated to the United States in 1917. He worked as a waiter in Boston before he was admitted to Penikese on May 25, 1919. Wing was nicknamed "Jimmy." and was among the patients transferred to Carville in March, 1921, and died there in 1934.[19, 26, P]

Case #40. **John Marketakois,** 24. Immigrated from Greece in 1911. He lived in this country for eight years and was sent to Penikese on November 8, 1919. Marketakois had a sister in Greece, who also suffered from leprosy. There is a record indicating that Dr. Parker may have sent medications to Marketakois's sister.

Marketakois was transferred to Carville and escaped from there in November, 1921, and was not heard from again.[19, 26, P]

On May 9, 1920, *The Boston Post* ran a news item which said a man named William Comber of Narranganset Pier had been leprous for 25 years and had not left his house for the last five years. When he was discovered, he escaped with his family to New York. This man was never officially recognized as leprous by health officials and so no number was given to him.[P]

In 1920, four cases were sent to Penikese and not assigned a case number by the Board of Charity. For ease of identification the author has assigned a number to each of the following cases:

Case #41. **Frank Lena** (a/k/a Frank Santo Taosone), 24. Single. Born in Italy and immigrated to the United States. He settled in Rome, New York, where he worked in a candy factory. Lena was sent to Penikese Island on January 22, 1920. He was transferred to Carville in 1921, escaped later that year, and was readmitted in 1931. While assigned to the Carville hospital, Lena was married. Frank Lena died at Carville in 1938.[26, P]

Case #42. **Nicholas Bruno.** Born in Italy. Out-of-state resident. He was employed in Baltimore, Maryland as a "cement worker" and may have lived in Brooklyn, New York for a time before being to sent to Penikese on February 1, 1920. He was transferred to Carville in 1921 and then was discharged to Brooklyn, New York in April, 1929.[26, P]

The last two cases were veterans of World War I. These two men had been in many hospitals around the country for several years. The U.S. government asked the Commonwealth of Massachusetts to accept them at Penikese. A special law was introduced in the Massachusetts Legislature and voted on at once to accept them.

Case #43. **Getulio L. Avelino**. Native of the Philippines. He was a member of the United States Navy when he was diagnosed with leprosy. Avelino was sent to Penikese in April, 1920, and discharged from the service on June 18, 1920. He was transferred to Carville in 1921 and escaped four months later. He was readmitted November 24, 1922, and escaped again on February 15, 1923, and was never heard from again.[20, 26, P]

#44. **David Ernsberger** (a/k/a David Palmer), 22. Born in India, where his parents were American missionaries. He lived there until he went to college in Ohio. At the outbreak of World War I, he quit college in his junior year to join the United States Marines. While stationed in France, he became ill and was later diagnosed with leprosy. Ernsberger was sent back to the states, stayed at various hospitals, and in April, 1920, was the last patient to be admitted to the Penikese Island Colony. He was transferred to Carville in 1921 and escaped in October, 1922. In August, 1923 he was readmitted and escaped again 12 years later. He was again readmitted on May 5, 1939 and died 17 days later. While assigned to Carville, Ernsberger was married to another patient. He and his wife were allowed to live in a small cottage on the hospital grounds.[20, 26, P]

References for
Reported Cases of Leprosy

1. Proctor, J.W., *American Journal of Public Hygiene*, "Leprosy in Mass.," Vol. XV11, No.1, Feb. 1907, pp. 88-91.

2. Kalisch, Philip A., *Bulletin of the History of Medicine*, "Tracicie and Penikese Leprosoria." John Hopkins University Press, Baltimore. Vol. XLV11, No. 5, Sept-Oct. 1973, pp. 491-508.

3. *Harwich Independent*, Harwich, Mass, Nov. 22, 1905.

04-19. Numbers indicate year of Board of Charity Annual Reports, State House Library, Boston.

12A-19J. Indicate year and month of Monthly Reports of Parker, on file under Wolbach Papers, Francis A. Countway Library of Medicine, Boston.

24. Dept. of Vital Statistics, Boston.

25. Report of the town clerk of Gosnold, Cuttyhunk, Mass.

26. Author's private correspondence with U.S.P.H.S. on July 12, 1978 and Aug. 8, 1978.

28. *The Times*, April. 3, 1915, Col. B. London.

29. *The Star*, "Flashbacks," U.S.P.H.S, Carville, La.

37. *New Bedford Standard Times*, "Bourne Man A Leper," Dec. 12, 1915.

P. Marion Parker's personal scrapbook, Francis A. Countway Library of Medicine, Boston.

The Penikese Island
Cemetery

The Island Cemetery is located behind a hill about 500 yards north of where the leper cottages had stood. This was considered a good place for a cemetery because the patients could not see it from their living quarters. When a patient died, the body may have been placed in quicklime so it would deteriorate rapidly. It was feared that natural decomposition of the body would allow the disease to infect the soil and then spread to animals and humans.

The graves were marked with wooden boards, which were about eight inches wide, several inches thick, and about 18 inches high. The deceased's initials and an official number were carved into the boards and records were kept to show which number and initials belonged to which patient. By 1932, the boards had rotted away and were replaced by small oval-shaped cast iron markers, numbered and initialed as the boards had been.

Over the years, some of these markers have been moved and others have been lost. The Penikese Island School had duplicate markers made of cast aluminum to replace those that were lost. Unfortunately, there are no longer any records to indicate which person is buried in which grave. The exceptions to this are the graves of Goon Lee Dip, Nicholas Cacoulaches, Lucy Peterson, and Isabelle Barros. Their graves are marked with small granite gravestones. The cemetery continues to have a green picket fence around it as it did when it was first established, though the fence has certainly been replaced.

There was little thought given to natural erosion when the cemetery was first established. The corner of this burial area now lies close to the edge of an embankment. At the present rate of erosion, the graves will be exposed by the middle of the twenty-first century.

In 1981, the Cuttyhunk Historical Society felt that Dr. and Mrs. Parker had not received enough recognition for their work on the island. This society, with the aid of the Penikese Island School and Richard Nickerson of Orleans, placed a plaque on a natural stone near the entrance of the cemetery. The plaque reads:

This monument is erected in honor of
Dr. and Mrs. Frank Parker
who for fifteen years (1907-1921)
directed the care of the patients
of the Penikese Island Leprosarium

Patients Buried in This Cemetery
John Roderick - 1907

Joseph Needham - 1913
Frank Pina - 1914
Archibald J. B. Thomas - 1915
Isabelle Barros - 1915
Morris Goldblatt - 1915
Iwa Umezakia - 1916
Walton E. Keene - 1916
Solomon Goodman - 1916
Lucy Peterson - 1916
Yee Toy - 1917
Nicholas Cacoulaches - 1920
Goon Lee Dip - 1920
Julia E. Lowe - 1920

Erected by
Cuttyhunk Historical Society, 1981

Janet Bosworth of the Cuttyhunk Historical Society (left) and the author (right) unveiling the monument on Penikese in honor of Dr. Frank and Marion Parker

Endnotes

Part 1

1. Elizabeth Reynard, *The Narrow Land*, Houghton Mifflin Co., The Riverside Press, Cambridge, 1934, pp. 29-31.
2. Frank R. Lattin, Ed., as quoted in *Penikese, A Reminiscence*, Albion, NY, by the author, 1895, pp. 56-57.
3. Lauermann and Burke, *Rhodora. Journal of the N. E. Botanical Club*, "The Flora of Penikese Island" Vol. 78, No. 816, Oct. 1976, p. 708.
4. Barbara Blau Chamberlain, *These Fragile Outposts*, The American Museum of Natural History, The Natural History Press, Garden City, NJ, 1964, p. 127.

Part 2

1. Edward F. Gray, *Leif Eriksson, Discoverer of America*, Oxford Press, 1929, pp. 122-124.
2. IBID, p. xiv.
3. Louise T. Haskell, *The Story of Cuttyhunk*, Reynolds Printing, New Bedford, MA, 1953, p. 14.
4. Gabriel Archer, *True Relations of the Voyage of Bartholomew Gosnold, 1602*, as quoted in Amelia Forbes Emerson, *Early History of Naushon Island*, privately printed, 1935, p. 34.
5. IBID, p. 38.
6. Haskell, *The Story of Cuttyhunk*, p. 14.
7. Catherine Marten, *Occasional Papers*, "The Wampanoags in the 17th Century." Plimoth Plantation, Plymouth, No. 2, 1970, p. 3.
8. IBID, pp. 5-14.
9. Haskell, *The Story of Cuttyhunk*, p. 4.
10. Frank G. Speck, *Indian Notes and Monographs, #44*, Heye Foundation, 1928, p. 115.

Part 3

1. Lloyd C. M. Hare, *Thomas Mayhew, Patriarch of the Indians*, D. Appleton Co., 1932, pp. 84-85.
2. Alice Forbes Howland, *Three Islands*, privately printed, 1964, pp. 4-5.
3. Herbert A. Wilcox, *Daniel Wilcox of Puncatest*, privately printed, South Pasadena, California, 1943, pp. 22-39.
4. Henry Howland Crapo, *Certain Comeovers*, privately printed, New Bedford, Vol. 1, 1912, pp. 332-342.
5. Howland, *Three Islands*, p. 101.
6. IBID, pp. 102-103.

7. James Freeman, *Massachusetts Historical Collection*, 1807, Second Series, Vol. 3,1807, p. 78.
8. *Tisbury Vital Statistics*, Births pp. 44, Deaths pp. 214-215.
9. Daniel Ricketson, *History of New Bedford*, privately printed, 1853, p. 378.
10. David Starr Jordan, *The Days of Man*, World Book Co., Yonkers-On-Hudson, NY, Vol. 1, 1992, p. 114.
11. Correspondence of Charles Patchelder, Boston, February 24, 1964.
12. Howland, *Three Islands*, p. 104.
13. *The Evening Standard*, New Bedford, June 11, 1903, p. 10.

Part 4
1. *The Evening Standard*, "History of Penikese," New Bedford, July 6, 1905.
2. *Harpers Weekly*, "Penikese Island," August 9, 1873, pp. 701-702.
3. Anonymous, *In Memoriam*, J. Howard Brown, NY, 1882, p. 4.
4. *The Evening Standard*, "Penikese", New Bedford, April 22, 1873.
5. IBID.
6. Louise Hall Tharp, *Adventurous Alliance*, Little Brown, 1959, p. 233.
7. IBID.
8. Frank H. Lattin, Ed., *Penikese, A Reminiscence*, Albion, NY, 1895, pp. 23-24.
9. *Organization and Progress of the Anderson School, Report of the Trustees for 1873*, Cambridge, p. 2.
10. Lattin, Ed., *A Reminiscence*, pp. 30-31.
11. Arnold Guyot, *Memoir of Louis Agassiz*, Princeton, 1883, p. 46.
12. G. R. Agassiz, Ed., *Letters and Recollections of Alexander Agassiz*, Boston, 1913, p. 130.

Part 5
1. Alice Forbes Howland, *Three Islands*, privately printed, 1964, p. 111.
2. Dukes County Courthouse, Records Department, Edgartown, MA.
3. Lida C. Lowry Brannon, *A Trip to the Site of the Agassiz Laboratory*, paper read to Biological Club, November 1895, Student University, North Dakota.
4. IBID.

Part 7
1. State Board of Charity, *Annual Report*, 1915, p. 85.
2. IBID, p. 90.
3. *Boston Globe*, September 2, 1910.

Part 8
1. Editorial Board, *Massachusetts Physician*, December, 1964, p. 78.
2. State Board of Charity, *Annual Report*, 1915, p. 94.
3. Private interview with Miss Alice Dobbyn, October, 1977.
4. Department of Vital Statistics, Boston, MA.
5. *Boston Journal*, "Woman Leper Cured", September 8, 1906.
6. Private correspondence with Dorothy D. Reiss Barros, March, 1997.

Part 9
1. Private family records loaned to author.
2. Hyman Small, *The Star*, "An Old Timer Remembers," U. S. P. H. S. Carville, LA, July, 1944, pp. 3-10.
3. State Board of Charity, *Annual Report*, 1907, p. 69.
4. *Annual Report*, 1907, p. 69.
5. IBID, p. 70.
6. IBID, p. 72.

Part 10
1. State Board of Charity, *Annual Report*, 1908, p. 97.
2. IBID.
3. IBID.
4. Unidentified newspaper, "Girl All Alone on Big Liner," NY, May, 1912.
5. *Annual Report*, 1908, p. 98.
6. State Board of Charity, *Annual Report*, 1909, p. 100.

Part 11
1. *Boston Sunday Post*, "Woman Braves Leprosy for Love of Her Son," April 4, 1909.
2. State Board of Charity, *Annual Report*, 1909, p. 99.
3. Unidentified newspaper, "Raving Leper as Passenger," October 24, 1909.
4. IBID.
5. *Annual Report*, 1909, p. 101.

Part 12
1. *New Bedford Times*, "New Hospital for Penikese Lepers," August 4, 1910.
2. State Board of Charity, *Annual Report*, 1910, p. 93.
3. Correspondence, Office of Postmaster General, March 8, 1979.
4. Sandrick, W.A., *American Philatelist*, "Disinfected Mail," April 1986, pp. 334-348.
5. State Board of Charity, *Annual Report*, 1911, p. 56.

Part 13
1. Unidentified newspaper, "Penikese Leper Colony Afire."
2. State Board of Charity, *Annual Report*, 1913, p. 62.

Part 14
1. State Board of Charity, *Annual Report*, 1912, pp. 59-61.
2. IBID, p. 60.
3. *Boston Sunday American*, "Leper Patients Leave Penikese," January 18, 1914.
4. Private correspondence of Dr. S. B. Wolbach, May 9, 1952.
5. *The Standard*, "Leper on Cars," New Bedford, September 18, 1913.
6. *Boston Herald*, "Even Lepers Joyous at Christmas Time," December 1913.
7. Dr. J. A. Honeij, *Report to Board of Charity*, November 29, 1913.
8. Unidentified newspaper, "Claims Chinese Leper Was Not Cured of Disease," Boston, Jan. 17, 1914.

Part 15
1. Bailey, Rev. Nathan, "Carrying the Word of Cheer to the Lepers at Penikese" *The Sunday Standard*, New Bedford, May 18, 1919.
2. IBID.
3. *Boston Sunday Globe*, "Heroism on Penikese," May 23, 1915.
4. State Board of Charity, *Annual Report*, 1914, p. 57.
5. *Boston American*, "Boy Leper Thanks American Readers," Sept. 20, 1914.
6. *New Bedford Mercury*, "Clever Work in the Leper Colony," Aug. 31, 1914.
7. *Annual Report*, 1914, p. 58.
8. *Boston Herald*, "Government Seeks Penikese," Dec. 22, 1914.

Part 16
1. *New Bedford Sunday Standard*, "Stays in Leper Colony," Feb. 21, 1915.
2. *The London Times*, April 3, 1915, p. 3, Col. B. London.
3. State Board of Charity, *Annual Report*, 1915, p. 73.
4. IBID, pp. 95-96.
5. State Board of Charity, *Annual Report*, 1916, p. 69.
6. Division of State Adult Poor, *Penikese Hospital Report*, Nov. 25, 1916.
7. Division of State Adult Poor, *Penikese Hospital Report*, Feb. 24, 1917.

Part 17
1. Sisters of Charity, *History of the Louisiana Leper Home*, Carville, LA, p. 13.
2. IBID, pp. 4-14.
3. Division of State Adult Poor, *Penikese Hospital Report*, Dr. Frank H. Parker, June 30, 1917.
4. Commonwealth of Massachusetts, *Bureau of Vital Records*, 1917, Gosnold.
5. Division of State Adult Poor, *Penikese Hospital Report*, Oct. 27, 1917.
6. State Board of Charity, *Annual Report*, 1917, p. 58.
7. State Board of Charity, *Annual Report*, 1918, p. 51.
8. Division of State Adult Poor, *Penikese Hospital*, Frank H. Parker, Feb. 28, 1919.
9. Department of Public Health, *Penikese Hospital*, Pub. Doc. #34, 1920, p. 219.
10. *The Sunday Herald*, "Army Lepers Find Home Here," Boston, April 25, 1920.
11. Hyman Small, *The Star*, "An Old Timer Remembers," July 1944, p. 3.

Part 18
1. Unidentified newspaper, "Pathetic Scene as Lepers Are Put on Train."
2. *New Bedford Sunday Standard*, (No Title), Dec. 28, 1920.
3. *New Bedford Standard*, (No Title, No Date), p. 30.
4. *Boston Sunday Post*, "No Reward for Friend of Lepers," March 20, 1921.
5. Author's private correspondence, Marylyn Sturdivant, U.S.P.H., Carville, LA.
6. Unidentified newspaper, "Dr. F. H. Parker Dies in Montana."
7. Author's private correspondence with Robert Parker.

Part 19
1. Correspondence on file, Massachusetts Div. of Fisheries and Wildlife, Westboro.
2. Chap. 477, Sect. 1, Massachusetts State Legislature, 1924.

3. Alice Forbes Howland, *Three Islands*, privately printed, 1964, p. 117.
4. IBID, p. 118.
5. Correspondence on file, Massachusetts Div. of. Fisheries and Wildlife, Westboro, Dec. 29, 1924.
6. Correspondence of Div. of Fisheries and Wildlife, Aug. 31, 1925.
7. Correspondence of Div. of Wildlife, Nov. 23, 1926.
8. Correspondence of Div. of Wildlife, (No Date).
9. Howland, *Three Islands*, p. 118.
10. Correspondence on file, Div. of Fisheries and Wildlife, Mar. 25, 1926.
11. Correspondence on file, Div. of Fisheries and Wildlife, (No Date).
12. Howland, *Three Islands*, p. 118.
13. Private interview with James McDonough, Div. of Fisheries and Wildlife.
14. IBID.
15. Private correspondence, Jame D. Lazell, Jr., Feb. 13, 1979.
16. C. B. Floyd, *Bird Banding*, Dept. of Interior, Vol. 111, 1933, p. 173.
17. Lauermann and Burke, *Rhodora, Journal of Botanical Club*, "The Flora of Penikese Island," Vol. 78, No. 816, Oct., 1976, p. 707.
18. Floyd, *Bird Banding*, p. 174.
19. Correspondence on file, Div. of Fisheries and Wildlife, July 10, 1934.
20. Private interview with David Masch, Penikese Island, Dec. 10, 1978.
21. Court records on file, Dept. of Wildlife.

Part 20
1. Private interview with George Cadwalader, Woods Hole, Jan. 1970.
2. Penikese Island School, *Annual Report*, 1973-1978.
3. George Cadwalader, *Castaways*, Chelsea Green Publishing, 1988, pp. 8-10.
4. IBID, pp vii-xi.
5. IBID, p. 173.

Selected Bibliography

Chamberlain, Barbara Blau. *These Fragile Outposts.* Garden City, NJ: The Natural History Press, 1964.

Emerson, Amelia Forbes. *Early History of Naushon Island.* By the author, 1935.

Cookin, Warner F. and Barbar, Philip. *Bartholomew Gosnold, Explorer and Planter.* London: Archon Book, 1963.

Gray, Edward F. *Leif Eriksson, Discoverer of America.* Oxford Press, 1929.

Hare, Lloyd, C. M. *Thomas Mayhew, Patriarch to the Indians.* NYC: D. Appleton Co., 1932.

Haskell, Louise T. *The Story of Cuttyhunk.* New Bedford: Reynolds Printing, 1953.

Howland, Alice Forbes. *Three Islands, Pasque, Nashawena and Penikese.* By the author, 1964.

In Memoriam. NY: J. Howard Brown, 1882.

Lattin, Frank R. Ed. *Penikese, A Reminiscence.* Albion, NY, 1895.

Lazell, James D. Jr., *This Broken Archipelago,* Quadrangle, New York Times Book Company, 1976.

Marten Catherine. "Occasional Papers in Old Colony Studies." *The Wampanoags in the Seventeenth Century.* No. 2, Dec. 2, 1970. Plymouth, MA: Plimoth Plantation, Inc., 1970.

Massachusetts Board of Charity. *Meeting Notes, 1904-1910.* Boston: State House Archive.

Massachusetts Board of Health. *Annual Report, 1920-1921.* Boston: State House Library.

Reynard, Elizabeth. *The Narrow Land.* Cambridge: Houghton Mifflin Co., 1934.

Index